NOT MADE
for DEFEAT

Dr. Oswald J. Smith

NOT MADE
for DEFEAT

The Authorized Biography of Oswald J. Smith

by

Douglas Hall

With a Foreword by Dr. Billy Graham and
an Introduction by Dr. John Wesley White

*"Man is not made for defeat. Man can
be destroyed but not defeated."*

A. E. Hotchner
"Papa Hemingway"

OLIPHANTS

OLIPHANTS
BLUNDELL HOUSE
GOODWOOD ROAD
LONDON S.E. 14

First British Edition 1970

ACKNOWLEDGMENTS

Gratitude is expressed to the following for permission to use their copyrighted poems and hymns:

Page 95 — "Deeper and Deeper" Copyright 1914. Renewal 1942 by Oswald J. Smith. International copyright secured. Assigned to Zondervan Publishers.

Page 113 — "A Revival Hymn" Copyright 1933 by Homer A. Rodeheaver. International Copyright Secured.

Page 176 — "The Glory of His Presence" Copyright 1935 by Homer A. Rodeheaver. International Copyright Secured.

Page 177 — "God Understands" Copyright 1937 by The Rodeheaver Co. International Copyright Secured.

Page 177 — "The Song of the Soul Set Free" Copyright 1933 by The Rodeheaver Co. International Copyright Secured.

Page 178 — "Then Jesus Came" Copyright 1940 by The Rodeheaver Co. International Copyright Secured.

ISBN 0 551 00228 X

Printed in Great Britain by Compton Printing Ltd London and Aylesbury

FOR PAUL SMITH

Dr. Smith and Dr. Graham, 1968

FOREWORD

There are some men of God who are called to minister the Gospel to a city, others to a nation; and a few in each century to the whole world. As a missionary statesman, pastor, evangelist, Bible teacher, author and hymn writer, Oswald J. Smith is a prophet to the nations of the whole world. Above anyone of the twentieth century, he has probably done more as a missionary statesman, to recruit workers for the foreign fields and to inspire the prayers and financial support of Christians everywhere to sponsor the implementation of our Lord's Great Commission. On repeated and protracted itineraries, he has himself gone to the ends of the earth with the Gospel, and where he has not been able personally to go, his words on radio and television, and his pamphlets, books and hymns have communicated the Gospel of Jesus Christ, whom he so deeply loves. His life is a shining example to young and old throughout Asia, Europe, Africa, South America and the Islands of the sea, as well as across the British Isles and his native North America. And what is more remarkable is that this ministry has spanned two generations and shows no signs of waning.

He has been one of my close and trusted friends for nearly 30 years. When I began preaching, he encouraged and inspired me, and as I said recently in The Peoples Church, on the occasion of celebrating his sixtieth anniversary as a preacher of the Gospel, through the years he has been a constant tower of strength and valued counselor to me. And I know of few father-son combinations in the ministry who have formed such an effective team for proclaiming the Gospel as he and his son, Paul. In a world where the church is losing its grip, to see a church which is attended by nearly 4,000 people each Sunday, gives over a third of a million dollars annually to foreign missions, and has been blessing people in Toronto and around the world in this way for over 40 years, is surely one of the Christian miracles of our time.

BILLY GRAHAM

INTRODUCTION

It is a most felicitous undertaking for me to write a word about Douglas Hall's *Not Made for Defeat,* for Douglas Hall is my favorite novelist and there is no Canadian alive for whom I have such utter admiration as for Oswald J. Smith.

Dr. Smith has worn the varying hats of missionary statesman, unexcelled founder and longtime minister of the largest church congregation in Canada, and distinguished author of 35 books.

Even at this writing, he is thousands of miles away evangelizing and holding conferences on world evangelism — as he is so incessantly doing.

Douglas Hall is fast emerging as one of Canada's most prolific novelists, writing at the rate of approximately one book a year — and there is no end in sight.

In *Not Made for Defeat* he does not grasp the pen of a mere hagiographer. All of us who have known Oswald J. Smith casually or intimately know well that he is an outstanding man of God. He prays as few men pray. He preaches with a fervor, compassion and clarity which could be found in few others today. He also lives a holy and singularly devoted life.

It takes, however, someone such as Douglas Hall to show us that Dr. Smith is also immensely human, loves humor, and is a devoted husband and father. He is as good a neighbor as he is a world missionary statesman.

Any biography of Oswald J. Smith would sell. This one will sell and be read with increasing enthusiasm as the pages are turned.

Toronto, Canada   JOHN WESLEY WHITE D. PHIL. (OXON)

Billy Graham Associate Evangelist,
Chancellor of Richmond College, Toronto

The Smith family:
Paul, Mrs. Smith, O. J. Smith, Hope and Glen

PREFACE

In dealing with the life of such a man as Oswald J. Smith, the easiest and probably most predictable approach a biographer could take would be to credit the man's every accomplishment to God and every failure to some unseen force.

This book will not be a work of deification, however, for if it were, it would not be the story of Oswald J. Smith. Rather, it would be just a narration of what God has accomplished through one man.

There will probably be many readers who will look for constant acknowledgments to God for everything this man has achieved during his long and remarkable career as a minister of the Gospel.

I will take this opportunity to state, and only once, that "Oswald J. Smith undoubtedly is one of God's chosen servants who asks nothing for himself, but to serve, and gives God all the praise and the glory."

Having stated this, I shall now make an honest attempt to tell the story of a man who is recognized by both his advocates and detractors as being a legend in his time.

This book could not have been written without the gracious help of many people. To them, I extend my sincere appreciation for the countless hours they have spent telling me what they know and think about Oswald J. Smith: the man; the minister; the hymn writer; the author; the missionary leader; the husband . . . and the father.

To list each one by name would be impossible. There are, however, five who I would like to publicly thank, Dr. and Mrs. Oswald J. Smith and their children, Glen, Hope and Paul.

DOUGLAS HALL

Oswald & Ernie, Hazel & Alice with their parents in the year 1898.

The old Embro Station
where Smith spent his boyhood
(later renamed Zorra)

Chapter 1

The years between 1889 and 1895 were called by historians "Canada's Age of Discovery."

The routine way of life in Canada was finally undergoing change after decades of discovery and settlement.

Interwoven across the country was a web of gravel roads which brought families together. The roads made it possible for small towns and hamlets to come alive, at least on Saturday nights, as men and women, boys and girls, mingled with horses and buggies for a "night on the town."

There were new wonders to see during those memorable years. Electricity was being demonstrated in some store windows and the highlight at the Canadian National Exhibition, in Toronto, was the new electric street railway.

Men of vision and accomplishment were making their marks in the world. Sir Sanford Fleming had a plan to split the world into time zones. They called it Standard Time.

Education was broadening its field of influence. Up to that period in Canadian history, it was practically a necessity to live in one of the larger towns or cities if one wanted to obtain a formal education. Now, the farmer's children were becoming educated no matter where they lived in the Dominion.

The schools were often red, and nearly without exception, had only one room. The teacher, who either lived in town or boarded at a nearby farm home, had to stoke the pot-bellied stove and teach all eight grades.

It was truly the beginning of the twentieth century because many of Canada's leading figures in politics, the arts, the professions and religion today began their careers in the spartan educational surroundings at the turn of the century.

Just such a man was Oswald Jeffrey Smith. The eldest of ten children, six boys and four girls, he was born to Benjamin and Alice Smith on November 8, 1889 in a modest farmhouse on the outskirts of Odessa, a small hamlet in southern Ontario.

"Ben" and Alice Smith were celebrating their second wedding anniversary when young Oswald was just four weeks old. Celebrations of any kind in Canada during the 1880's differed greatly from what they are today.

"We were fortunate," recalled Oswald years later. "Since my father was a telegraph operator for the Canadian Pacific Railway and had a steady income, sometimes nearly $40.00 a month, we never went without. We weren't 'dirt poor' but we sure weren't rich. I don't know what they had to celebrate that second anniversary, but knowing my mother there would be a special treat of some kind, even if it was just a fresh orange, something we children got once a year in our Christmas stocking."

The life of a railway man is nomadic. For the first few years Oswald and his parents, plus the other children who came along, moved like gypsies from Odessa, to Walkerville, to Woodstock and finally to Embro in the lush rolling countryside of southwestern Ontario in 1893.

Embro, where the CPR stationhouse was located, and Cody's Corners a mile and a half down the road, where the red brick school stood at the crossroads, have held a strong attraction for Smith down through the years. He returns whenever possible as he tries to recapture the joys and sorrows of his boyhood.

Cody's Corners was named after relatives of William F. "Buffalo Bill" Cody. One of his distant cousins, Andrew Cody, recently retired from farming and still lives on the homestead. Andrew and Oswald were boyhood chums and have kept in close touch down through the years as both near their eightieth birthdays.

"I remember it as if it were yesterday," said Oswald as he pointed out a spot in the schoolyard to a visiting friend. "I stood right there and played baseball with my classmates."

Leaning his tall, angular frame against the red bricks of

the school house he closed his eyes in reflection. "How warm it feels in the afternoon sun. Many times this was the only place that was out of the cold. We would huddle here waiting for the bell to ring so we could go back into the classroom. There were many violent pushing bouts for the choice spot."

"Did you ever push anyone so you could get the place?" he was asked.

His face broke into a smile, "Sure I did. I was a boy once, just like the rest."

For the first ten years of young Oswald's life he grew up like any other country boy. There were always new trees to climb, new mysteries to solve and new adventures to fill his days.

If time ever hung heavy on his hands he could usually find something to do or see around the station. Trains chugged in and out and the conductors soon came to know the tall, thin Smith "lad" as they came into the station to receive orders or check the manifest lists.

Life was never dull.

His boyhood chums, many long passed into the oblivion of time, were a part of those early years. Andy Cody was one who vividly recalls their early life at school.

"We played the usual games, baseball in the spring and fall and scrub hockey in the winter," he recalled. "Oswald was not an especially athletic lad, even though he tried to take part. I can remember that he played a fair game of ball and because he was so tall we used to think it gave him an advantage over the others. He had an exceptionally long reach. You never saw anything until you saw him make a hit and run the bases. When we used to eat lunch he would climb one of the large maple trees and drape his legs over a branch. That was his lunch counter."

The mile and a half to and from school held many attractions. There was a small creek which, when swollen by the spring rains and melting snow, became a virtual torrent. The temptation was generally too great for schoolboys to resist. More than once the air was rent by the anguished cry of an unwary victim who had reached out too far after a frog or floating branch. One such occasion provided Oswald the opportunity to be the hero of the day.

"The creek was swollen from heavy rains and Mother warned us to stay away from it and come straight home. I realize now that it went in one ear and out the other, at least that day it did. The place was alive with frogs and as the girls watched from the road I and the rest of the boys began catching them. Suddenly, without warning, one of my friends fell in and it was at a spot which was over his head. I waded out and because I was taller than the others was able to grab him and drag him in. I don't know now whether he would have drowned or not, but he swallowed a lot of water. Instead of being scared all he could say was, 'I lost my frog.' His name was Osborne McKenzie. He was killed in the first World War."

It was shortly after that episode that Oswald faced one of the most searing moments of his life, one that was to leave its mark and have a significant influence on his later years.

Anyone who knows him as a minister is familiar with his motto "no attack, no defense." He has withstood personal attacks down through the years without ever answering back, even in self defense.

Probably that attitude stemmed, in part, from the time a local bully stopped him on the way home from school and tried to pick a fight. When the challenge was refused the boy's clenched first flew through the air and caught young Oswald square in the eye.

"I don't remember his name and to the best of my knowledge never saw him again. I honestly don't know why he wanted to fight me. I wasn't an aggressive boy, in fact I don't think I ever picked a fight with anyone."

The black eye scarred his personality more than it showed because he has always, since that day, had a fear of physical violence.

The Smith family was well respected in the community and a degree of this respect can be attributed to their upbringing. Ben Smith was a hard-working, honest man who instilled a strong sense of self-respect in each of his children. His high standards became the family hallmark.

Unlike many children of today most youngsters growing

up around the turn of the century had to pitch in and shoulder their fair share of the work load. If they lived on farms there were cows to milk, byres to clean, and stock to feed. For Oswald the chores took on a different cast, but were nevertheless wearisome.

The station house was his field of labor. It had to be swept out and tidied up. This included filling the woodbox and cleaning out the pot-bellied stove. He also had to trim, clean and light the semaphore lamps each day.

Smith has retained a deep respect for his father who he remembers as kindly, indulgent and at times, perhaps overly permissive.

"I can only recall two times when father ever let his emotions get the better of him and resorted to physical punishment. The first time was when I was disobedient and forgot to come home in time to light the semaphore lamps. The other occasion was when I hitched up a stray Great Dane to a sleigh and gave my sister, Hazel, a ride which could have resulted in her getting severely injured.

"Anyone who knows anything about railroading realizes that engineers will not pass an unlit semaphore light. They are required by law to stop the train and find out why the light is out before going on, so Father's actions were understandable.

"Hitching the dog to the sleigh was a foolish thing to do, but at the time I thought it would be fun since the dog was nearly as big as a small horse. I put Hazel on the seat and they were off. My sister hung on for dear life. The dog went berserk. Having never been in harness before all it could think of was getting away. Finally after what seemed like an eternity the sleigh upset, Hazel was thrown out and a runner was broken off.

"Those are the two times that I can ever remember my father laying a hand on me, and for that matter, any of my brothers or sisters."°

It's only natural that an animal was involved in this escapade because ever since Smith was a young child animals

---

° Smith followed his father's example in bringing up his own children. Under certain circumstances, he believes that there is a place for spankings, but he never subjected any of his three children to anything more than minor corporal punishment. Despite being on the verge of exasperation on numerous occasions he held himself back and resorted to lecturing the dissident in his study instead.

and birds have played important roles in his life. He had many pets as a boy, including hundreds of rabbits and white rats. His special love, however, was a black crow which he and his brother Ernie took from a nest during one of those rare adventures which are commonplace to country boys.

The crow, which he called "Tommy," quickly adapted to domestic life and was soon the talk of the neighborhood as it began learning words and phrases from its patient master. Years later Smith rekindled the memory of his pet crow with an aviary of exotic birds in his home.

As childhoods go the Smith children were relatively fortunate. Their parents, Victorian though they may have been, loved their children and kept their best interests at heart. The home atmosphere was made as pleasant and congenial as possible, so much so, that each one recalls with fond memories their formative years.

"Father," said Oswald, "was the head of our family and cherished his position with one exception. Mother had been a Christian from the time she was a young girl, but Father didn't make a real profession until years later, long after the children had left home to make a life for themselves.

"Mother took up the slack and performed her duties as spiritual head to the best of her ability. Whatever I learned as a child I learned from her, as church for us was usually a hit-and-miss affair."

Whenever it was possible the family would go to Embro and attend the local church and Sunday school. From time to time an itinerant minister would hold special meetings in the schoolhouse or church and they would attend if the opportunity arose. It was a four mile walk to the town so unless there was a ride in a buggy or wagon the family stayed at home.

From his earliest recollections Oswald had been interested in God and the Bible. On more than one occasion he would warn his younger brothers and sisters to be careful how they acted because someday they would want to go to heaven.

His father's laissez-faire attitude toward religion didn't take an aggressive form. He never objected to Oswald's leanings in that direction. In fact, on one particular occasion he was the means of bringing the gospel message right into the home.

The local town drunk, a man called Richardson, had come under conviction and did a complete about-face. Instead of scrounging drinks and spending most of his waking hours in a stupor, he began holding prayer meetings in nearby farmhouses. This intrigued Oswald who hurried about to finish up his chores so he could attend and take an active part in the meetings. All the while, he didn't have a clear understanding of what salvation really meant.

Oswald could hardly believe his ears when his father gave permission to Richardson to use the station waiting room for his meetings. From then on, every Sunday night Oswald sat in rapt attention, as he listened to the Gospel being presented in the simplest of terms, practically in his own living room. Despite constant exposure to the straight-forward message and an intense interest, he was not converted at that time.

Not all of Oswald's earlier years were pleasant. From the time he was born his mother, especially, had a deep-seated concern for his health. A tall, gangling child, he never really seemed to fill out. More than once there was serious doubt as to whether he would ever reach adolescence.

Reminiscing one day he said, "I contracted a severe case of pneumonia and despite the fever kept on trudging the mile and a half to school. It isn't fair to blame my parents for not getting proper medical attention when I first developed the illness because doctors were scarce and home remedies plentiful. I remember seeing the classroom swim before my eyes, then everything went black. They tell me I fell backwards and cracked my head. In any case, I wasn't to return to classes for two years during which time many visitors had written me off. It was generally accepted that I hadn't many more days on this earth.

"I wonder what people would say if they could see me now?"

In retrospect, there were three major traumas in Oswald Smith's early life: the black eye; the whippings by his father, and the death of his oldest sister Hazel. Each one left its mark and in many ways have come to the surface during his career as a minister.

Hazel is buried in the small cemetery on the hill overlooking Embro. Oswald tells of the events leading up to her death as he stands by her grave on one of his numerous visits. His mother and father lie alongside their daughter in the Smith family plot.

"If you have ever had a fourteen-year-old boy in your home you can appreciate how absolutely obnoxious they can be, especially toward their brothers and sisters. Imagine what they are like and how they can tease and you will have a pretty good idea of what I was like at that age. I taunted Hazel unmercifully, getting great delight from seeing how far I could go before she would begin to cry, or I'd be told to stop by Mother or Father. Up to that point in my life she was just my sister, a girl to tease. Looking back on it now I regret many of the things I did, including the frequent clouts which I gave her when I was sure no one was looking and I could get away with it.

"My attitude abruptly changed when suddenly she became ill. Mother sent for Dr. Green, the family physician in Embro, who diagnosed her condition as a chronic heart ailment and ordered complete bed rest. For the first time in my life I really missed her. I can't honestly say for sure whether it was the playmate I missed or the target for my unmerciful jibes, but nevertheless I missed her. For a time she rallied and after an extended convalescence was soon playing, limitedly though, with her brothers and sisters.

"A short time later she was in bed again, this time for good. Dr. Green wanted consultation and called in a specialist from Woodstock, about six miles away. The prognosis was not good. My parents were told that it was doubtful if she would ever get better.

"This had a profound effect on the family, particularly Mother and Father. The children knew that she was deathly sick and went out of their way to be gentle and kind to each other.

"I began to have pangs of remorse. At the first opportunity I sat by her bedside and asked her to forgive me. Her reply was all that I could have asked for, 'I don't mind.' With those three words she erased the burden which I'm sure would have weighed me down long after her death had I not been able to make things right.

"It was only a matter of time. As we kept watch at her bedside we saw a bit of Mother and Father die along with their daughter who slipped away at the age of ten years."

Ministers are supposed to be born to griefs and joys, but no matter how long it has been, Oswald never conducts a funeral service without remembering, fleetingly, his little sister's death.

Smith at the age of 14, with brothers and sisters. Hazel, the sister who died, is in dark dress sitting on arm of chair

Mr. and Mrs. George Billings
(Daisy Smith's parents)

Ben and Alice Smith, Smith's parents

Chapter 2

In a feature story on the life of Oswald J. Smith, which appeared in a September 1968, issue of the Toronto *Daily Star*, Religion Editor Allen Spraggett quoted Smith as follows: "It is obvious that God has chosen Billy Graham for a special role. There was only one John Wesley in his day. And there is only one Billy Graham. God makes the choice."

Between the years 1902 and 1906 God apparently made an exceptional choice. Reuben Archer Torrey and Charles McCallon Alexander formed the most effective international evangelistic team ever seen up to that time in religious history.

Torrey's powerful preaching and Alexander's masterful musical ability drew capacity crowds as the two girdled the globe holding crusades in Australia, Tasmania, New Zealand, India, England, Scotland, Ireland, the United States, and Canada.

Travel was a trial rather than a luxury in those days as it was not uncommon for packet steamers to take literally months to round the Cape of Good Hope from England. Torrey and Alexander's accomplishments were all the more remarkable because of the distance they covered and the results their combined ministry reaped.

A small railway station at Embro is a far cry from the bustling hub of the Empire in London, but nevertheless the paths of two great evangelists were soon to cross that of Oswald Smith, then an impressionable youth of sixteen.

The highlight of the day at Embro came when the baggageman threw a roll of Toronto daily papers on the station platform. Everyone present from hangers-on to section hands eagerly grabbed a paper, sat on one of the benches and devoured the daily news. One of the most avid readers was Oswald, especially when he saw references to evangelistic meetings which were drawing over 3,000 people and noteworthy enough to make the front pages.

He had never heard of Torrey or Alexander — in fact, he had never been in a real evangelistic meeting in his life. The closest he had come to meaningful preaching was during Richardson's waiting room services. What his meetings lacked in finesse he made up for in sincerity. Instead of 3,000 there would probably be no more than six to ten at any one service.

Oswald was fascinated. He could hardly grasp what it would be like to hear such men. The singing alone would be enough, he thought. In one story, the reporter had featured the words and music to one of Alexander's hymns which seemed to have caught the ear of the thousands in attendance. It was called "The Glory Song."

Words such as conviction and conversion began appearing in the accounts of the meetings — foreign words to Oswald because he didn't have the faintest idea of what they meant in context.

The meetings were the talk of the countryside. The people who lived around Embro were basically God-fearing folk who had a common interest in religion. They discussed the pros and cons of the various concepts openly and generally without rancor.

The more they talked the more Oswald listened. For the first time in his life he had an insatiable curiosity about religion, especially the type being preached by Torrey and Alexander.

Travel was a luxury in those days and not to be undertaken at any great length without due consideration. Even a trip to Woodstock, six miles away, was an event worthy of planning.

Oswald wanted to go to Toronto. He knew that if he could count on his brother Ernie for moral support there might be a chance.

For hours they talked it over and planned. Their father wasn't a problem. If their mother agreed, they knew he would go along with whatever she said Finally they approached

24

their mother. All the answers to any questions they thought she might ask were firmly fixed in their minds. To their surprise she agreed to their going. She even went so far as to make arrangements with their Aunt Phoebe in Toronto, to put them up and keep an eye on the two young adventurers.

It was more than they had ever expected. It had really been too simple. They were sure that it was going to take arguments and counter-arguments to convince their mother that they were grown up enough to be allowed to travel to the big city, over ninety miles away.

As the two boys boarded the train and looked back to wave good-by the thought flashed through Oswald's mind that being the son of a railroad man had its advantages. In spite of the cleaning and lamp lighting he knew that he'd probably never have been able to go without the free train pass.

Massey Hall was the cultural mecca of Toronto. Practically every renowned artist of the day, from Jenny Lind to Enrico Caruso, had performed on its stage. Its acoustics were legendary in North America and everyone who appeared there sang its praises.

It was a gift to the city from the Massey family, which is internationally known and respected in agricultural equipment manufacturing, the arts and politics. A vital link in a chain of public auditoriums, it still serves Toronto's public well.

"I was glad that Ernie and I were able to get our first impression of Massey Hall the way we did," said Smith years later. "As we stepped off the streetcar we saw the crowd jamming the sidewalk and pouring over into the street. We had no intention of being trapped at the end of a long line so decided to push our way to the front. We wanted to be among the first in and get a choice of seats.

"It's amazing what two determined boys can do when they want to go somewhere. If we had been older we'd probably never have gotten away with it. Being kids, we were able to elbow our way through the people and get practically up to the door. After a wait of nearly half an hour the doors opened and we were literally swept into the building. The first glimpse was overwhelming. The stage was so big I thought it would probably hold Embro with room to spare. We just stood and stared. Suddenly it was as though someone had turned on a giant tap. People poured into the main floor and balconies which stretched around three sides of the auditorium. Instead of rows of empty seats there was a sea of expectant faces. Ernie and I quickly grabbed two seats before they were all gone. As it was, hundreds were turned away, not able to get in.

"Years later when I would stand on the platform and conduct evangelistic services I'd look for the two seats that my brother and I sat in and wonder if the people in them were experiencing the same sense of excitement we did that day so long ago."

If anyone has ever felt the thrill of seeing a childhood hero in real life they will understand how the two Smith boys felt when the door to the stage opened. The under-current of conversation died down and Charles Alexander walked out followed by his accompanist, Robert Harkness.

They were not disappointed. He smiled, nodded in the direction of the piano, raised his arms and led the packed auditorium in one rousing hymn after another, including his now famous "Glory Song."

For the next eight services the boys sat transfixed as they came under the spell of Torrey's overpowering oratory which had made him famous around the world. They both decided to go forward when the invitation was given following the seventh service.

Conversion is the most personal thing in anyone's life and the best person to tell exactly what happened is the one involved.

"It was an afternoon meeting, a special one for boys and young men only. Ernie and I got there early as we didn't want to take a chance of getting locked out. It was a good thing we did because the building quickly filled. I often wonder in later years who could draw 3,400 boys and young men to an afternoon evangelistic meeting? If there was anyone it would be Billy Graham, but somehow I think even he'd have difficulties in this day and age.

"I can't honestly recall what Dr. Torrey said that day, but I'll always remember his text, Isaiah 53:5 . . . 'But He was wounded for my transgressions: He was bruised for my iniquities, the chastisement of my peace was upon Him, and with His stripes I am healed.'

"That was enough for Ernie and me. At the close of the message Dr. Torrey began to give the invitation. It was different from the usual, all-encompassing one I had expected. He began with the 25-year-old group and worked his way down the age ladder. By the time he came to my bracket I was numb and just sat there. Why I don't know. A jab in the ribs from Ernie jolted me to my feet and I went forward to shake Dr. Torrey's hand. I was directed to the counseling room in the basement and a personal worker began talking to me.

"I've preached over 11,000 sermons in my career so I guess I've seen every kind of conversion there has been. Some just look straight ahead and remain passive, others break down and go through an emotional experience, while some walk out of the counseling room the same way they walked in. For a while I thought I was going to be one of the latter. Nothing happened. The worker left me, probably thinking that I'd made a clear-cut decision, but I hadn't.

"Suddenly the tears began to flow and I knew without doubt that my sins were forgiven and I was a child of God for all eternity. There wasn't any particular excitement, no sudden surge, just the quiet confidence that I would never have to wonder again about where I'd spend eternity. I now had God and He had me."

Oswald's brother Ernie also went forward that afternoon. He later became known as the Reverend E. Gilmour Smith, a minister with the United Church of Canada in Peterborough, Ontario.

Both boys learned sometime later that their mother had written to Dr. Torrey asking him to pray with her that her sons would be saved during the meetings.

Smith (standing at left) 1908
with Indians of British Columbia

Lumberjack preachers
in British Columbia, 1919
(Smith is in centre)

Lumber camp
in British Columbia
as Smith saw it

Chapter 3

No matter how sympathetic friends and relatives may be to religion or church, they always seem to hold a new convert at arm's length and somehow manage to ask such ageless questions as:

"Is it for real?"
"Do you think it will last?"
or
"I wonder what made him do it?"

For Smith, it was a lonely time following his return from Toronto. His mother was overjoyed that her prayers had been answered and went out of her way to help and encourage her two boys. Unfortunately, she could not offer what they needed most — solid grounding in the Word of God. Sincere as she was, she just didn't have the necessary training or background to help new converts. There wasn't a spiritual mentor around for them to lean on and look to for guidance.

Many times Smith has used his early experiences as a neophyte to encourage others who might tend to waver because they have to face their new life as a Christian all alone.

"I firmly believe," he has said, "that if a conversion is real, it doesn't matter where the new Christian is or what the circumstances are. If he is sincere, he will remain true to his commitment to Christ."

Those first days were difficult ones. Smith wanted desperately to serve, but didn't know how to go about it. He only had his mother, brother and Bible for comfort. Night after night, after his chores were finished, he would read his Bible by the flickering light of a coal oil lamp. Questions would grab his mind, but there was no one he could ask for answers. His brother didn't know any more than he did and their mother was unable to discuss anything beyond the basics of Christianity.

His desperation to serve provided the courage to tell some of his classmates and teacher that he was now a Christian. This was really his first attempt at reaching others with the Gospel.

Every child, especially a boy, goes through phases. At one time or another they want to be either a fireman, railroad engineer or ship's captain, but not young Smith. He can never remember wanting to be anything except a preacher. The trip to Toronto galvanized that desire in his subconscious.

Until his experiences at Massey Hall he just wanted to be a preacher. However, seeing Torrey in action and watching the effects of his oratory on those listening, convinced him that he wanted something more. He just had to be an evangelist!

This yearning for a goal became his one thought day and night. As he walked along the right-of-way to light the semaphore lamps he would preach out loud the sermons which were in his heart. Torrey's platform gestures were mimicked, but instead of an appreciative audience of 3,000 such as Torrey addressed, there were only a few birds and chipmunks to see and hear the tall kid who sang and preached his head off. He may have apeared comical, but it was deadly serious business . . . he wanted to serve God.

His mother, with the special understanding that mothers have, knew her son was going through troubled times. In quiet desperation she offered to help him start a Sunday school in the station waiting room. This was better than nothing and Smith grasped at the suggestion. His every free hour was spent visiting families in the area and inviting the children to attend classes on Sunday.

It's impossible to be in Oswald Smith's presence very long and not be conscious of his restless nature. He seldom sits still for any length of time. Rather he stalks back and forth as he talks. His pent-up energy was evident even as a small boy and young man.

"I've been asked many times," said Andrew Cody, "if I

can remember what Oswald was like as a boy. The best answer I can give to anyone asking is to tell them to go to church and watch him on the platform. Some ministers stand still, face their congregation and preach in a quiet, reserved manner — but not Oswald. He moves about, jabbing with a finger to emphasize a point, waving an arm to keep attention or thrusting his jaw forward at a crucial moment in his sermon. It's as though he is impatient with himself and his audience. He always appears to have so much to say and regrets the limitations of time. That's exactly what Oswald was like when we went to school together — impatient, restless and always on the move."

This restlessness came dramatically to the surface shortly after Smith's conversion. He couldn't content himself with Embro and what it had to offer. Reluctantly his parents gave their consent for him to return to Toronto and find a job. Soon after his arrival in Canada's second largest city, he began working in the office of the Massey-Harris Company in the city's west end. His salary was the princely sum of $3.00 per week.

During the following months he became involved with a Hornerite congregation and went through one of the most difficult periods of his young Christian experience. He began to have doubts about his salvation.

The Hornerites were a body of sincere believers who accepted the Arminian doctrine of sinless perfection. They also taught that it was possible to sin your salvation away either knowingly or unknowingly.

Service after service Smith went forward to the altar pleading with God for salvation and assurance. The more he prayed the less secure he felt. His conversion was no longer real as he began to doubt everything he had held dear to his heart, only a few short months before.

As is so often the case when doubt assails young Christians, God always provides the answer, sometimes at the last moment. Smith's answer came in the form of a pamphlet someone gave to him called "Safety, Certainty and Enjoyment."

The title of the leaflet tells the story of what it contained and for well over sixty years it has been Smith's testimony. He's been Safe, Certain and filled with Enjoyment.

31

In a life filled with memorable experiences it's not surprising that this one has been related over and over. Smith continually tells new Christians that if they are truly converted they have nothing to worry about for all eternity. Once a person has gone through a period of doubt and has experienced the joy of assurance they do everything within their power to keep others from ever having to face what they had to experience.

Being the nephew of Thomas Findley, an executive of Massey-Harris, didn't make things any easier for Smith.

Findley had worked his way up through the company and before he retired he became president of the international farm equipment manufacturing organization. The Massey family who were responsible for Massey Hall, were also actively connected with the firm at that time. As is the case with most self-made men, Findley made sure that, relative or no relative, all employees worked hard and produced for the company.

Smith went out of his way to prove himself, but it was short-lived. His health, which was tenuous to say the least, broke down once again, causing him to faint on the job.

He was taken home where his aunt, Mrs. Phoebe Findley, immediately put him to bed and for the next few days nursed him back to a degree of health. Since his aunt was the wife of Thomas Findley and Smith was living in their home, there was no question about his taking advantage of his position. He was really ill.

It was obvious that he couldn't return to work so his parents were contacted and told he'd be coming home as soon as he was strong enough to make the trip.

During his son's absence in Toronto, Ben Smith had resigned as station agent at Embro. He left the Canadian Pacific Railway and joined the government-owned Canadian National Railway, the largest in the world. He became the first station agent at Mount Albert, a small town about 40 miles northwest of Toronto.

Mount Albert was much like Embro. In fact all small towns look somewhat alike. There was the usual string of small stores on the main street, one or two churches and a railway station right near the feed store and mill. Smith wasn't particularly interested in his new home. This is apparent as in later years when he mentions home he talks about Embro and Cody's Corners. Seldom does he ever mention the other places in which he lived.

Smith's mother took over where his Aunt Phoebe left off and nursed her son back to health and strength once more. When he was well enough, he enrolled in the first form at Mount Albert High School. This lasted for a few months until restlessness once more got the better of him. He returned to Toronto and a job in the office of the National Cash Register Company where he worked under a second cousin, Herbert Daly. His earning power had increased nearly 300 per cent as he was now making $8.00 per week. Oswald Smith had finally left home for good at the age of seventeen.

Smith's job at National Cash was just a stopgap. He was completely on his own and had to earn a living. His real interest was not in impressing his superiors. Rather it was in becoming a minister. He had spoken on one or two occasions to young people's groups in Mount Albert and at the Beverly Street Baptist Church in Toronto. These exposures to the public platform whetted his appetite. He was so desperate to appear before an audience that he even went so far as to address one organization concerning the ways and means of missionary work in Japan, a subject about which he knew absolutely nothing.

He explained the situation years later by saying, "I suppose that it was the drive to preach which overshadowed the lack of expertise I had in the subject. I've often heard young preachers address an audience and wondered if they really know what they are talking about or were they just doing what I did. It was good experience and instead of dampening my desire it only heightened it."

Since he had made the move to be completely self-sufficient, Smith didn't return to the Findleys to live. Instead he took a room in the heart of Toronto. He spent his free hours reading the Bible and biographies of outstanding men of God. He has advised countless new recruits for the mission fields or seminary students to read all the biographies they can. The best way he will tell them, to understand what God can do, is to read the life stories of men such as Alexander, Brainerd or Moody.

It was during one of his reading sessions that he came across a Toronto Bible College advertisement. T.B.C. was offering evening classes in Bible and Bible English. This was exactly what he had been looking for — sound teaching.

He enrolled immediately and began attending two nights a week. For Smith this was the pinnacle of pleasure and fulfillment.

During his days at Toronto Bible College there was a young lady who in her own way went on to public recognition as one of Canada's outstanding religious writers.

Jane Scott has been writing religion in Toronto for over 40 years — first as Religion Editor with the *Globe and Mail* and currently as syndicated columnist with the Toronto *Telegram*.

"I wasn't very impressed with Oswald as I remember him," recalled Miss Scott. "He was just another boy in college, a rather tall, thin boy.. I don't suppose I impressed him either, so I guess we're even," she smiled.

"To say that I'm impressed with him now is an oversimplification. He is a remarkable man. One only has to recount his achievements to realize that. Oswald Smith will go down in history as probably Canada's greatest evangelical leader. In the field of missions he has no peer."

During his student days at Toronto Bible College Smith honed his skills as a preacher by taking services wherever and whenever they were offered. These took him into one of the city prisons where he taught the Bible. He also spoke in rescue missions and pulpits where few established preachers would hold services. His church at that time was the Beverley Street Baptist Church. The minister, the Reverend William Wallace, took full advantage of Smith's energies and let him assist with a group of boys. His life had finally taken on meaning and purpose.

Smith's first real home church was Chalmers Presbyterian Church which he attended faithfully until one day he heard some discussion about a minister who was capturing the imagination of many people. His name was J. D. Morrow and

34

he was pastor of St. Mark's Presbyterian Church. Once Smith heard Morrow he was hooked. Morrow was a spell-binding preacher with a deep understanding of the Bible and the art of communicating with an audience. Morrow's ability was reflected in the success he had in just eight short months. When he took over St. Mark's the attendance was around thirty every Sunday. In just a short while it had grown to well over two hundred. This is all the more remarkable because St. Mark's was right in the middle of the lower working class area, the hardest group to interest in church and religion.

Smith was then, and has always been, attracted by people who can move and show results. He cannot tolerate the status quo. Morrow fitted his image of what a man of God should be and do. He left Chalmers and quickly joined St. Mark's.

Never backward about putting himself forward he asked if he could take an active part in the church program. He was given a class of small girls to teach. Smith was determined that they would be the best taught and best attended class in the church and within a short while they were just that.

It is ironic that his youthful idol, Morrow, was to become his colleague. It didn't happen over night, but Smith was destined to become Morrow's Associate Pastor before many years had passed.

Smith, prairie-chicken hunting
at Hollywood, Manitoba, at
the age of 20, in 1910

Smith in the mountains of Kentucky

Chapter 4

Even though Oswald Smith was just a teenager and a relatively new Christian it didn't take him long to realize that being a minister of the Gospel meant different things to different people.

For some it was a glamorous calling filled with prestige. The church had an air of respectability and was included with the professions, law and the military as ideal fields for ambitious young men. It was easy to spot the ministers who had entered the church just to please their families. At the turn of the century in Canada it was a mark of distinction to have a member of the family "serving the church." Usually the question of a definite call from God to serve was not considered.

For Smith these were lame excuses. He only had one answer when asked why he wanted to devote his life to full-time service.

"I don't question God's will, but I know that as sure as I'm alive I must preach the Gospel. There's nothing else in the world for me."

The classes at Toronto Bible College only fired his desire and he couldn't contain himself any longer. Without even considering the fact that not everyone felt as he did, he applied to the Presbyterian Church for a mission field appointment.

"I've never really considered defeat or failure," he once said. "No matter what I've attempted I've always gone into it with the utmost confidence. Don't get me wrong. I've had my defeats, probably more than my share if they were all

37

totalled up but they don't bother me. For the moment I would think that the world was dealing me an unfair blow. Now when I look back I'm grateful that I've always had the ability to put such things out of my mind and get on with the next task. You might call it rationalization. Whatever it was it helped me get over some rough spots. I always tried to concentrate on the positive aspects of a situation and thus keep a pretty clear perspective of what's been accomplished and what's ahead."

In 1908 Smith had the opportunity to put this philosophy into practice.

At that time, the Presbyterian Church of Canada, while being completely evangelical, was conservative and somewhat stodgy. Its leaders took their founders in Scotland as an example and acted accordingly. When Smith's application for an assignment was reviewed by the mission's board there was no hesitation on the part of the members to turn it down. Despite fervent pleadings by Rev. J. D. Morrow they rejected the application. Morrow obviously spotted something in Smith that prompted him to place his professional reputation on the line by recommending his acceptance. The Board thought otherwise. It was just not done, having a brash 18-year-old boy as a full-time field representative of Canada's most influential church. The file was closed!

"I've often wondered where I'd be now if they had accepted me. Probably in some staid, unexciting Presbyterian or United Church. When I look back on it and can see the radical change which has come over the Presbyterian and Methodist Churches following their amalgamation into the United Church of Canada. I'm sure I've been able to accomplish more in an independent work . . ."

With typical Smith logic he reasoned that if he was too young and inexperienced for the mission field he might as well start at the bottom and become experienced. The best way, he thought, would be to get into churches, meet people, preach and distribute the Word of God wherever possible. Selling Bibles seemed to be the answer.

The Upper Canada Bible Society's restrictions about who

would sell their product weren't particularly rigid. They were mainly interested in good salesmanship plus an earnest desire. In Smith they found both. He made application and without too much wrangling was accepted as a colporteur and sent to the Muskoka region of Ontario by Reverend Jesse Gibson, Secretary of the U.C.B.S.

The dictionary defines "colporteur" as "a hawker or distributor, especially of religious tracts or books." It could enlarge upon that definition to say that in Smith's case he was the forerunner of the Fuller Brush Man. Instead of brushes, waxes and cleaning preparations he was merchandising Bibles which ranged in price from a modest 12 cents for a hard-bound cloth volume to $2.00 for the leather bound top of the line.

While he might have been a door-to-door salesman his tactics were anything but hit-and-miss.

"I was very precise in my planning, I left nothing to chance. Everything was considered. I never went into a community without first making sure that I'd be welcome and, more important, successful. The first thing I did was to get accommodation. Many salesmen have been failures because they land in a new town and start off selling cold. I never did this. I'd find out who was offering room and board, eliminate the ones who charged over $3.00 per week and the ones who appeared to run a low-grade establishment. Any salesman worth his salt can get this kind of information within an hour of landing in town. Once I had my lodging I'd head for all the ministers and ask for their cooperation before I ever opened my case. Small towns have the greatest communications system in the world. I bet I wasn't in town half a day until word had gotten around that a Bible salesman had arrived. Contacting the ministers also gave me entrance to their churches. Most ministers welcomed a new face and if they could talk or had a story to tell, they'd be in the pulpit next meeting. I banked on this because I certainly could talk and had a story to tell. At least I thought I did when I was making my plans. It's easy to be over-confident if you've never had the opportunity to prove yourself. Having the minister publicize me and my Bibles from his pulpit opened many doors. This publicity helped me make my sales. I've continued that approach of getting complete cooperation from the local community or responsible individuals all my career. Many times I've found out how important it is to have the right people on your side, especially when city-wide crusades were being conducted."

The door-to-door salesman is only as successful as is his prowess with a customer. The product is secondary. A good salesman should be able to "sell refrigerators to Eskimos." If the product is exceptional and the salesman sincere, the sale is almost assured.

The U.C.B.S. had a winner in Smith. Not only was he a good salesman, he believed in what he was selling. As a result he sold more Bibles in the Muskoka area than any other salesman before him.

"I think I called on every farm house in the district. Sometimes I was welcomed warmly, other times indifferently. On a couple of occasions I had the door slammed in my face. Word of mouth had much to do with my reception. If you know what rural communities are like you'll realize that everyone on the party line knew I was in the district within minutes of my first call."

One of the compensations for growing old is the ability to reflect on a life filled with highlights and disappointments.

Usually the highlights overshadow the disappointments because memories are short when it comes to unpleasant experiences.

For the pilot it may be his first solo flight. The hockey player relives the thrill of his first National Hockey League goal. The doctor never forgets the surge of pride that gripped him as he delivered his first baby.

The minister?

Nothing can compare with that first sermon when he looked into the eyes of his congregation and poured out the sermon which God had laid on his heart.

In 1908 the village of Severn was a collection of modest houses clustered around the railway station as if seeking protection.

Strung down the dirt road which served as the main thoroughfare as well as the central artery of the community, were a few small stores, the blacksmith shop and the Severn Methodist Church. Its minister, the Reverend Elijah Brown, was a remarkable man. Not remarkable in his own sight but remarkable nevertheless. He was to play a significant role in the life of Oswald Smith.

Whenever the daily train disgorged its passengers and wayfreight each person and item was given a close going over by the local residents, who always seemed to appear from out of nowhere at train time.

Smith stood on the platform, tall, gaunt, unsure of what to do. Perched on the express wagon was an elderly man with a bushy mustache, parted by a yellow pipe stem. He uncrossed his legs and leaned forward to look at the stranger.

Before he completed his inspection the last person on the platform, besides Smith, crossed the old man's view and walked toward the young man.

"I'm the Methodist minister here, my name's Elijah Brown. First time in Severn?"

Smith shook the extended hand and swallowed hard, "Yes it is. I'm Oswald Smith."

The ice was broken and within a few moments Brown had learned that Smith was in the community on behalf of the Bible Society. He liked the boy immediately.

"Well then, let me have your bag. You'll have to stay somewhere, how about my house?"

As Smith looks back upon it, it was Divine intervention. With one or two exceptions, Smith's accommodation had always been provided or he was able to secure it reasonably at a local boarding house. He still recalls the night he had to sleep in a barley field because the customary farm hospitality was not forthcoming.

As they walked away from the station Brown questioned Smith closely about his background and work.

Suddenly he stopped, dropped the bag and looking at his young companion said, "Would you mind preaching for me tomorrow?"

It took Smith about as long as it takes a drowning man

41

to grab a life preserver to say, "Yes, I'll be glad to preach for you."

The chilling thought that Brown might ask about his preaching experience gripped him and he hung back for a moment.

His fears were well founded as Brown looked around and asked, "I suppose you have spoken before?"

Nearly on the verge of panic because he didn't want to miss the opportunity to preach for the first time Smith gulped, "Spoken, oh yes, I've spoken before."

He was correct because he had spoken before, twice at young peoples meetings. Fortunately Brown hadn't phrased his question to ask if he'd ever preached before . . . because he hadn't.

The answer seemed to satisfy the older man because without commenting on it further he asked in a very business-like manner, "I have three appointments: will you preach at all three?"

With the excitement and assurance of youth Smith replied, "Gladly."

It never occurred to him that he didn't have three sermons to preach. In fact, he didn't even have one.

The balance of the walk to the Brown home was filled with idle chatter about Bibles and how they were sold door-to-door. Following dinner the two men chatted a while longer, but Smith's mind wasn't on the topic of conversation. He was beginning to wonder seriously if he'd bitten off more than he could chew. It was fortunate for him that Brown had three appointments in his circuit because that meant there would be three different congregations, but there was a problem. Brown would be at all three services and Smith didn't want him to think that all he could preach was one sermon. He must have three no matter what they were.

Smith could hardly wait until he was shown his room and had the privacy of a closed door. Suddenly it came to him. He remembered hearing Reverend Elmore Harris, one of the editors of the Scofield Reference Bible, preach a sermon on Ephesians 1:3. "Blessed be the God and Father of our Lord Jesus Christ, who hath blessed us with all spiritual blessings in heavenly places in Christ." It was a deep, penetrating sermon and one which no minister should ever attempt unless he had at least 25 years experience in the pulpit. Smith was in no mood to justify his choice. Forgetting that he was embarking upon his career and had only a couple of minor experiences on a public platform, he decided to make this his first sermon. He had one thing in his favor, a fantastic memory. He closed his eyes and mentally mouthed Harris's sermon almost word for word. He even attempted some of the man's vocal inflections and mannerisms. Confident that he could get through the service he dropped off to sleep, forgetting one thing . . . he still had two sermons to prepare.

Sunday morning in the small Methodist church of Severn went better than Smith had ever dared hope. He spoke for nearly thirty minutes without a pause and absolutely no notes. Relying on his memory he was able to hold the unsophisticated country congregation's attention. Following the service Brown congratulated him on the sermon, little knowing that it was completely lifted from one of the most eminent and respected preachers of the day.

As they drove to the afternoon service at the small hamlet of Wesley, Smith sought desperately for a sermon topic. One verse of scripture after another came to mind only to be discarded for various reasons. He wanted, if possible, to make his second sermon as memorable as the first. As Brown rambled on about the differences between the Calvinistic and Arminian doctrines Smith was calling upon God for help.

"Dear Lord," he prayed, "help me to find the sermon You would have me preach."

His face lit up. "Yes, that's it," he blurted out. "John 3:14 to 15, 'The Serpent in the Wilderness.' That's my sermon."

"That's your what?" asked Brown.

"My text, John 3:14 to 15, I'm going to preach on The Serpent in the Wilderness."

Brown nodded, "Splendid, it'll do them good to hear a message on that."

The fastest way to get a minister panic-stricken, especially a new one, is to have a commotion or distraction take place

43

during his sermon. Smith was no different and that second service was his baptism in holding the attention of a congregation under trying conditions.

"Everything was going well. The people were attentive and secretly I was patting myself on the back. I was completely satisfied with my performance when it happened. The church was directly in front of the railway tracks and when the trains came by the very building shook, particularly if it was a long manifest freight going full speed. Off in the distance I could hear the train as it blew for a crossing. It didn't take but a moment for me to realize that I was in for it. I had two alternatives: I could either stop and wait for the train to rumble past, or I could keep on going. I decided on the latter. It must have been quite a sight, something like a silent movie. I never missed a word or a gesture, in fact I moved about and waved my arms more than normal to hold attention. The train drowned out every sound. The building shook, the platform shook and the congregation shook in their pews . . . I never missed a word. It passed almost as soon as it started and I modulated my voice to compensate for the fading commotion. As far as I can remember no one even gave a flicker of an eye to indicate that anything out of the ordinary had occurred. It was as though what had happened was completely commonplace."

That experience stood Smith in good stead in later years. One of his fortes as a minister has been his ability to hold an audience under any conditions. On many occasions this ability has paid off.

Washago was the final service and it was also the largest congregation of Brown's three appointments. Smith didn't have time following his two successes to revel in self-gratification, he had to come up with one more sermon and come up with it fast. It's no problem for an experienced minister to decide upon a sermon. Practically every one has a list of subjects which have proven acceptable and can be presented without a second thought. That's one of the main advantages of experience. Some decide long in advance what they will preach about, others wait until just before they step on the platform for a flash of inspiration picking the sermon to suit the audience. Whatever the practice it cannot be denied that Divine guidance plays an important part, especially if the minister is completely dedicated to his beliefs and role in life. If not, the selection may be simple expediency. Whatever it is, most congregations are seldom aware of just what goes into the planning of a sermon.

Smith has had to rely on both techniques. There was no question about his dedication and desire to serve God and there certainly was no question that dedication or not, he had to address his third congregation.

He thought "The Parable of the Ten Virgins" would be an acceptable subject so it became his final sermon of the day.

When Brown rose to introduce the visiting preacher he made mention of how this young man had blessed his two earlier congregations. He sincerely told the congregation that he was looking forward, with expectation, to what God had in store for them.

Smith could hardly believe his ears. All he had been trying to do was get through the three services without falling completely on his face. He'd never even considered the fact that he was blessing anyone.

The final sermon went smoothly, a little bit better than the second and still better than the first. Smith had arrived at the decision which was to affect his entire life. Up to that point he wanted to be a minister of the Gospel, but always he had the gnawing uncertainty of not really knowing whether or not he could make it. He didn't know for sure if he had the ability to hold the attention of complete strangers while he expounded his views on the Bible and the way of salvation. Now he had passed the point of wondering whether he would ever be a minister . . . he was one!

South Chicago Presbyterian Church, the second church Smith
served as student pastor, 1914 - 15

Chapter 5

It has been said that "success breeds success." For Smith this axiom proved true. His outstanding success in the Muskoka area evidently caught the eye of the right people. Upon his return home to Mount Albert following the end of summer, there was a telegram waiting for him from the Bible Society. They invited him to become their colporteur in British Columbia and open up the work on the coast. There was a west coast representative, but he mainly served as manager of the Vancouver retail store.

When Smith took over the Muskoka area, as far as he was concerned, it was only for the summer. He had definite plans to return to Toronto in the fall and enroll in the day-time classes at Toronto Bible College. The experience he gained in selling Bibles and meeting people was invaluable, and so was the money he earned. Without financial resources he could never expect to attend school during the fall and winter months.

It didn't take him long to accept the invitation. His decision was immediate.

"I fully realized the implications of the invitation, that's why I accepted so quickly and changed my plans," smiled Smith as he looked back on that turning point in his young life. "I wanted to preach more than anything else and I realized that here was my chance. If I was asked in Muskoka just a hundred miles from Toronto, what would it be like in British Columbia where ministers of any kind would be scarce? I'd probably sell Bibles, preach as often as I could, and make money in the bargain. It was ideal, I thought. I never considered the hardships — they were to come later."

British Columbia, Canada's most western province, has a coastline of nearly 1,000 miles with some of the most rugged grandeur to be found on any continent. Its heterogenous people range from the "Mayfair" Britishers who sip tea on the patio of Victoria's Empress Hotel to the Indian Sikhs who migrated from the Punjab to become the best loggers in the vast forests of the Pacific Northwest.

Smith probably knew less about British Columbia than many of the newly arrived Indians. He knew, however, that God was leading him there and this was all part of the overall plan which would fit him someday to fill his role as a minister of the Gospel.

Transcontinental travel in those days, while exciting, was not exactly the last word in comfort. The engines spewed smoke and grime back through the rattling cars where the passengers suffered in straightbacked, horsehair seats which were throwbacks to some distant reign of torture.

It was long before the days of plush Pullman cars and diners. If you wanted to eat during the trip you had to line up with the other passengers and wait your turn at the small wood-burning stove at the rear of the car. Once your meal was heated you hopefully made your way back to your seat with a half cup of tepid tea and a plate of partially warmed beans. Such inconveniences only heightened the excitement for the 18-year-old youth who had never been more than a hundred miles away from home in his life.

Every day brought new sights. The rustic forests of Northern Ontario gave way to the flat prairies of Western Canada. Beautiful as each region was, nothing could match Smith's first view of the Rocky Mountains. He couldn't take his eyes off the snow-capped peaks. This moving experience resulted in the beginning of a personal diary which he has continued for more than sixty years. To this day, he still records his observations and intimate thoughts as he travels about the world, preaching and holding missionary conventions.

"It was probably the Rockies which gave me the idea for a diary which has evolved as I've grown older. I wanted to be sure to remember all that had happened, the places I'd seen, and what I thought. It was also around this time that I started taking pictures, but the diary was more important. In those days people relied on word-of-mouth since television and films were really a thing of the future. It was only natural that as I went along I included more and more of my personal life with the descriptions of people and places. There were many times, especially in B.C. when I was all alone, that the diary nearly took on human characteristics. When you have no one to talk to and you're in a remote spot cut off from everyone, it's easy to understand how something like the writing of a diary can really become a personal communication. I didn't realize it at the time, but what I've written over the years has become invaluable background material for many of my sermons and writings."

With nothing to do on the train but read and watch the scenery pass by the window, Smith had plenty of time to write in his fledgling diary. Many of his observations are candid and vivid but in the case of his first view of the Rockies he comes across like an awed and overwhelmed teenager.

"The mountains are quite different from what I had expected. I was prepared for high snow-covered peaks, but find it impossible to fully describe the first sight of them off in the distance. It took us hours after we first saw them before we were really close. It was as if we were chasing the horizon. The most impressive moment was today when the train broke out of a tunnel into the blazing sunshine. It was as though we had suddenly come upon a fairyland world where everything was a glistening bigger-than-life setting for some gigantic theatrical production. I asked some of the passengers if it affected them the same way, but I couldn't find anyone who could improve what I'm writing."

The train journey took six days — the most exciting six days of his life. Over the years since, he has made the transcontinental trip many times, but nothing has ever compared to that first crossing of the prairies and Rocky Mountains.

Being Canada's main Western seaport, Vancouver, British Columbia, was also the gateway from the Pacific to the rest of the Dominion. Practically every nationality was represented in the mass of humanity which crowded the docksides and streets. There was a continual movement of people in and out of the port. They were either arriving from distant and exotic places or boarding some heavily laden steamer for Canada's far Northwest and an elusive fortune.

The Klondike "Gold Rush" in the Yukon Territory had burst wide open just twelve years before Smith's arrival in the West. The magnetism of gold drew prospectors and adventurers from all points of the globe until the Klondike eclipsed the famous California gold boom of 1849. The flurry subsided almost as quickly as it had begun and Vancouver, in the short space of just a few years, was turned into a mecca for the disappointed flow ebbing back to civilization.

Another "gold" was being mined in the flop houses, bordellos, sleazy restaurants and back alleys of the city . . . dope!

It has been proven that the introduction of illicit dope in British Columbia, and Vancouver in particular, can be traced to the influx of Orientals who floated in on the tide of excitement created by the "Rush." This segment of the population filled most of the menial jobs such as kitchen, laundry and maintenance help. These positions usually became the front for real professions as illicit peddlers of morphine, cocaine, marijuana and numerous other opiates. The drug situation had deteriorated so drastically that William Lyon Mackenzie King, a promising young public servant, was appointed by the Canadian Government to investigate the situation and bring back a report with recommendations to Parliament. King's investigation covered the period of Smith's arrival in Vancouver. Mackenzie King went on to greater prominence as one of Canada's outstanding Liberal Prime Ministers. Desperate as the problem was in 1908, there evidently wasn't any lasting solution because the Royal Canadian Mounted Police still consider Vancouver one of the major drug markets of North America, if not the world. It has become the supply depot for the insatiable demands of the American drug market.

Whether Smith realized it or not, this was the boiling pot into which he stepped as he left the train at the station.

One of the cardinal rules that itinerant preachers or full-time workers follow is to make sure that wherever they go they find out where the sympathic residents live. It provides the stranger two vital requirements, a point of contact and probably more important because of limited funds, gratis accommodation.

"Leaving the train station I decided to try and find Mr. and Mrs. Hitch," recorded Smith in his diary. "I had known them in Toronto's Beverley Street Baptist Church before they moved to Vancouver to study Oriental languages and then proceed to Tibet as missionaries. After walking some distance up Grenville Street I asked directions and following a short ride on a street car found their house. I was warmly received as I expected I would be. They invited me to stay with them as long as I was in the city and I gladly accepted."

It took Smith just two days to meet with the Society's west coast personnel and secure his supply of Bibles. A group of ministers formed the local committee and issued their youthful colporteur explicit instructions to make his way immediately to Prince Rupert and start selling Bibles.

As the *S.S. Camosun* threaded its way through Venn Passage in September of 1908 and entered Tuck's Inlet, which became the harbor of Prince Rupert, Smith elbowed his way to the railing. The deck was packed with as unlikely a cross-section of humanity as could be found anywhere. Chinese, with their hip length pig tails, vied for rail space with scarlet turbaned Hindus. Jostling right along beside were hard-bitten Europeans eager to gain a glimpse of what they hoped would be their new home and gateway to fortune.

Prince Rupert was just two years old, having been founded in 1906 by a small working party who hacked away at the heavily wooded shoreline until a foothold was seized.

The first real attempt at objective description in Smith's diary occurred when he made this entry the first night he was ashore:

"Prince Rupert is a small, lively place. It's to be the terminus of the Grand Trunk Pacific Railway and teems with hard looking woodsmen and railway workers. It has a splendid harbor with a long, deep channel where vessels can be completely sheltered from storms. Everything is new, the land is hilly and many of the town lots are posted for sale. The village has two streets, one a center street running straight back from the wharf and another running parallel with the shore. Both streets have a set of rails on which small cars are run to carry supplies up from the boats. The cars are drawn by a steam engine which is positioned at the end of each line. I didn't notice any horses about so I suppose this is the power they use to move things. Most of the houses are frame with a canvas covering. There are many tents all over the place and I think they must be pretty cold in the winter. I was told that the tents are only supposed to be temporary but like all temporary things they have a way of being permanent. I am surprised to find four churches established, a Presbyterian, Methodist, Episcopal and Roman Catholic. This pleases me because it means that there must be a number in the community who either support the churches or are sympathetic. I got talking to one of the local residents and he told me that I'd better be prepared to get wet because it 'rains here six days a week and pours on the seventh.'" Smith was soon to find out how true these words were!

Since Prince Rupert was just two years old and virtually squatted on virgin land it had an air of pioneering ruggedness. The trees, which had so shortly before rimmed the shore of the inlet, were now four foot stumps upon which planks were laid to form the streets. There were about six hundred permanent residents in Prince Rupert and to a man and woman, each one was as rugged as the surroundings. Most were hard-working, hard-drinking, hard-living individualists. They had no time for the niceties of life simply because the niceties were years away from arriving in their town. Strangely enough, as hard as they were, they appeared to have an underlying respect for religion. This was evident from the establishment of the four churches in just two short years.

Reverend Mr. and Mrs. M. Kidd earned themselves a niche in Prince Rupert's history. Mr. Kidd was the first Presbyterian minister and many of the early settlers crowded into his canvas covered plank chapel. It looked more like something children

52

had thrown together as a club house than a church, but never-theless, the Word of God was faithfully preached each Sunday by one of His finest servants. Kidd may have been short on pulpit skills and polish, but he certainly wasn't short on faith and sincerity.

Smith was invited to stay with the Kidds in their small home which stood beside the church. This became his center of operation as he called on practically every home and construc-tion camp in the area, selling Bibles. He repaid their kindness by preaching for Mr. Kidd. It's almost ludicrous to say he repaid him because he was doing what he wanted most to do, preach God's Word. One can imagine though, how grateful Kidd must have been to be able to introduce a new voice in the pulpit.

As Smith moved about the community and surrounding territory he encountered all kinds of receptions. Some were warm and friendly, some indifferent, and others, actually hostile and insulting to him personally and the product he was selling. These rebuffs only sharpened his ability to communicate, an ability that has never left him.

Knowing Smith's reluctance to become involved in physical violence of any kind it's difficult to imagine him as a duck hunter or hunter of any kind. One hunting trek nearly ended his brief but promising career.

"Mr. Kidd had told me about a few construction camps six or seven miles up the coast and suggested I take his row boat and see what I could do with the Bibles. I wasn't too anxious to go alone so asked a young fellow I had met to go with me. Mr. Kidd gave me his shotgun and recommended a few spots which he said were sure places for ducks. I wasn't much of a hunter simply because I never really liked killing anything. Ever since I was a child I could never stand to see an animal or bird hurt, let alone kill one. This was different. I was among people who killed for food and everything took on new meaning.

"During the trip up the coast my friend and I practised our hunting skills. As we came upon a flock of ducks in the water or flying near the boat we'd let go. Because they were not especially gun-shy we were able to get right up to them

53

before they took off. We got quite a few. Some were only grazed and these we let go once we were sure they were not seriously injured. I often wonder now how I could have shot them, but once I got over the initial shock of seeing something fall after I'd pulled the trigger, it became sort of fun.

"We worked our way up the coast calling on the scattered camps and homes. I sold a few Bibles and made a number of contacts. Some didn't do me much good but I hoped they might benefit Mr. Kidd or the other ministers at Prince Rupert. The people at least now knew about the churches in town and probably paid them a visit at some time or another.

"Following our last call my friend and I started back, keeping an eye out for some ducks. We wanted to bring a string home to Mrs. Kidd. She was an excellent cook and we could almost taste the plate of roast wild duck.

"As we rounded a point on the shore, about a quarter of a mile out we came upon a flock and began shooting. After the smoke had cleared and the ducks taken off we rowed over to where one was flapping in the water. The bird was badly wounded and we were sure it would die any moment. Not really knowing what to do we both sat and watched it flop around on the bottom of the boat. Realizing that it should be put out of its misery we tried different ways to kill it, but weren't successful. Finally, I decided to finish it off once and for all . . . I nearly finished the both of us off as well. I picked up an oar and brought it down on the duck's head with all my might. I not only killed the duck, I rammed the oar right through the bottom of the boat. A geyser of water broke through and began to fill the boat.

"My friend and I were terrified. We looked about and saw that there was a small island about a quarter of a mile away. Swimming for it was out of the question because the ocean was far too cold and we were heavily clothed. Fortunately I had struck the bottom near the side, rather than dead center. We shifted our position and were able to raise the boat in such a way that the hole was partially out of the water. I began rowing for dear life as my friend held his hand over the hole. We finally beached the boat and were able to plug the opening sufficiently enough to get us back to Prince Rupert."

Realizing that his potential sales had been exhausted, Smith decided to move along to new territory at Port Essington some thirty miles down the coast. Port Essington was as rugged as Prince Rupert and Smith captured the feeling in a poem he wrote called: "The Sunset."

> Great, mighty monarchs of the distant West
> That raise their lofty peaks to Heaven's crest,
> And in majestic splendor stand alone
> In one unbroken mass of rock and stone;
> Their snow-clad peaks now gleaming in the sun,
> Now lost amid the cloud that hangs like one
> Of God's great blankets of protecting care,
> Then lifts, and lo! again the brilliant glare
> Of sparkling snow on mountains far and near
> Beneath the setting sun so bright and clear —
> Proclaim that some great mind must overrule,
> And he who sees it not is but a fool.

The poem contains three verses, each one reflecting the intimate thoughts of a youth, thousands of miles away from home. He is not there because he especially wants to be, but because he was driven by an inner force to serve his God no matter what the cost.

Reverend and Mrs. C. B. Freeman, the Methodist missionaries to the Indians of the Port Essington district, invited Smith into their home and treated him as one of the family. Mrs. Freeman took a special interest in her guest and became a substitute mother to him during his stay.

For the next few months, Smith sold Bibles and preached to the Indians. Many times he traveled by boat to remote villages and was welcomed warmly by the local missionaries and Indians. He began picking up some of the Indian language called Chinook and this enabled him to make his sales pitch more effective. His Bible sales were encouraging, and better still, he was gaining confidence in preaching and communicating with an audience, even if it was Indian. Because of his limited knowledge of the dialect he was introduced to preaching through interpretation.

Winter was settling in with a vengeance and by Christmas Smith realized that it would be impossible to continue his colportage work. That Christmas was his first one away from home and he experienced a severe bout of depression and homesickness.

During his travels in the area he met a Reverend G. H. Raley, a Methodist missionary who was eager to have the young man as an associate and who offered him the winter post as missionary to the Indians at Hartley Bay. Smith accepted and secured his supplies which included: $20.00 worth of food; a small cook stove; an axe; a hammer and nails; two quilts and a blanket; plus fifteen jars of fruit and jelly.

As the small coastal tug *Princess Mary* pulled into the wharf at Hartley Bay a sudden wave of panic came over Smith. The village was almost hidden by deep snow and about as bleak and barren as anything he had ever seen. He was greeted by a group of stoic Indians who, after leading the way to the mission house, left him alone. The snow was so deep that he had to shovel his way in. The deepest drifts were well over five feet high.

Getting into the house was the easiest part of what was to follow. Smith always recalls that winter as the most uncomfortable and difficult of his life. The Indians were long on promises and short on action. It was their responsibility to keep the mission home supplied with dry wood and this was agreed to at an early meeting the chiefs had with Smith. What followed were days of soaking clothes and nights of bitter cold as Smith fought with his stove in a desperate effort to keep the green wood burning and his small quarters warm. The Indians were agreeable to anything he wanted so long as they didn't have to put themselves out. He organized a Sunday school, preached two services on Sunday plus four weekly meetings as well. Despite the personal inconveniences and bitter cold those winter months, while difficult almost beyond endurance, were also the most rewarding spiritually. The remoteness and complete isolation from other whites drove Smith closer to God as he spent his working hours in prayer and meditation. This experience undoubtedly fashioned his sincere understanding and empathy with missionaries and their problems in the years to come.

His work with the Indians was rewarding and despite their indifference to the sufferings which might befall a non-Indian, they were receptive to the things of God. This receptiveness overcame any feeling of resentment their missionary might have experienced.

Through sheer desperation and the will to better his personal comfort Smith gradually caught on to the ways of bleak pioneering. By the time winter had finally set in he thankfully had resolved the problem of wet firewood and was beginning to feel relatively secure in his surroundings.

In addition to his missionary work he taught the Indian children at school. Each day brought new experiences as he quickly warmed up to his charges and began to feel he was being accepted in the village.

By the end of April the warming sun of spring had opened up the country once more. Smith packed his meager belongings and left Hartley Bay to resume his work selling Bibles for the Society. For the next five months he traveled up and down the coast of British Columbia by boat, preaching in churches, mission halls, and streets — and selling Bibles.

Wanting to further his education and feeling that he had a good grounding in the field of missionary work with the Indians, he wrote a letter to the President of Manitoba College in Winnipeg. He stated his experience and asked for guidance in picking a suitable course of study. Dr. A. Baird replied that he could be accepted in the Minister-Evangelist course which would ultimately lead to the ministry in the Presbyterian Church of Canada.

In the meantime he had been offered a pastorate in the Methodist Church. This was an interesting offer, one which would have been snapped up just a short time earlier in his career. After intense prayer and personal evaluation Smith decided that he needed additional theological training in a recognized school so he chose Manitoba College.

"In looking back I've never been sorry that I turned down a pulpit in deference to more schooling. Preaching was my one desire. In spite of this, I realized my limitations and knew I was not sufficiently trained or educated to cope with a pastorate. The only time I ever chaired a business meeting was with the Indians at Hartley Bay. How could I ever expect to run a church and deal with a board without being at least moderately trained? I often question the wisdom of some who get saved, and before you know it, are calling themselves ministers and have their own church. Some might be successful but as far as I'm concerned there is nothing, with the exception of a Spirit-filled life, that benefits a minister more than sound academic and theological training."

Smith's decision launched him on a phase of his life which was not only to bring him stature in the eyes of his contemporaries, but was to affect the lives of countless thousands who have been touched by his ministry over the years.

Chapter 6

September 27, 1909, was a Monday. It had been exactly one year, two weeks and three days since Oswald Smith had passed through Winnipeg, Manitoba, on his way to British Columbia and the Indians.

This time is was different. No longer was he the wide-eyed youth, gaping at every new sight and sound. He was a seasoned missionary who had, in the short space of just a few months, gained stature as a man and as a Christian. Because of the many nights spent in the cold, lonely solitude of his forest cabin he had drawn closer to his Lord as he sought desperately for guidance and a deeper meaning to his spiritual life. As close as he felt he was to God in the wilds of British Columbia, he still had plenty to learn. His decision to attend Manitoba College in Winnipeg was a prime example. Excellent as it was, it was not the place where he should have gone. This was soon evident.

"It's a wonder that God ever kept patience with me. I was so determined and headstrong to serve Him that all I could think of was what I was going to do, not what God wanted me to do. I remember it so well. One night at Hartley Bay after days of personal conflict about my future I slid to my knees and prayed that oft-repeated cry, 'Lord, what wilt Thou have me to do?'

"I stayed on my knees for what seemed like hours, then got into bed, completely exhausted because praying, real praying, is hard work no matter what anyone says.

59

"I can hear it yet — the answer came as audibly as if another person were in the darkened cabin. 'Go to The Toronto Bible Training School.' It was the answer to my prayers. Why then did I enroll in Manitoba College instead? I don't know. If I did I'd consider myself to be one of the wisest men alive. One of the high points in my Christian life resulted from that experience. I was permitted to realize graphically exactly what being in the Will of God really means. For that I'm grateful."

Smith should have known quite quickly that something was amiss. Nothing really went smoothly from the moment he stepped off the train in Winnipeg. Not that being a Christian is the end-all to trouble. On the contrary, sometimes it's just the beginning.

It is easy to understand Smith's bitter disappointment just one week after his arrival. Following an exchange of letters with the College he was led to believe that his application to the special five-year course would be acceptable. Instead, the admissions board ruled him ineligible, offering instead the full nine-year course.

"I received one of the greatest disappointments of my life," he wrote in his diary on October 8, 1909. "The committee said that I couldn't take the course unless I put in a year on the mission field. They refused to recognize my work in British Columbia because I was not under the Presbyterian Church at that time."

Smith didn't know what to do. It was with mixed feelings that he viewed the possibility of spending nine years in study to emerge with only a Bachelor of Arts degree. He had nothing against formal education except the length of time it took out of one's life. He couldn't reconcile nine years when there was so much he wanted to do. It may have been youthful impatience, but it chafed to have spent a year in the wilds of British Columbia as minister, missionary and teacher, only to have it written off as not significant just because it wasn't sanctioned by a particular denomination.

His impatience is almost parodoxical because in later years his advice to young, enthusiastic converts is crisp and pointed: "Get a sound education, preferably at one of the fine Bible

Schools or Christian Colleges in North America. This is vital before starting out on a ministerial career."

Smith was once asked what he considered the major tragedy of the ministry to be. His reply was not what one would expect. He wasn't too concerned about the ministers who had fallen from the faith or the ones who lost their pulpits because of indiscretions. He was desperately sorry for the ones who were long on ambition and short on training.

"Years ago when I was starting out," he said, "anyone who had reached grade eight in school was well-educated. Now, university degrees are commonplace both at home and in the field. This includes most of what we used to call the backward African and Asian countries. With programs such as the Colombo Plan and other international educational schemes, many nationals are well educated, if not better educated, than some of the missionaries sent over to convert them to Christianity. It's sad to see someone become discouraged and leave full-time service because he was not properly trained either academically or theologically. Nothing can get a minister down so quickly as being written off because a communication gap arises between himself and his congregation."

Another area which touches on this problem has concerned Smith for years. In one of his books he devoted a complete chapter to "Training for Service."

He makes a strong case for those who are converted later in life and want to serve. Many are turned down because they are too old for formal academic or Bible training. He places the responsibility right before the missionary societies and Christian colleges, claiming that because of their set rules and requirements they are weakening their impact on the foreign fields. Missionary service should not be circumscribed by a lack of schooling or Bible training he believes, and he cites his career as a case in point.

"I was not a great academic student and have never considered myself an intellectual. Because of poor health and a less than desirable aptitude for 'book learning' I might never have achieved any degree of success in my chosen field if I had been required to master such courses as languages, mathematics, social sciences, chemistry or physics. I'm not downgrading these subjects because they are very necessary and should be mastered, but some people, including myself, just don't have ability in that area. I always excelled in English literature, but that was because I liked it.

"Mission fields, besides requiring skilled and professional personnel, also require dedicated Bible teachers. These are people who love the Lord and have a deep understanding of the Word of God. This understanding comes from a life of prayer and Bible reading — not in any classroom. Why can't these people be used?

"If a more liberal and flexible attitude were taken in this area I firmly believe that, instead of a lack of missionaries, there would be an ample supply for all the fields of the world. This would permit the missionary societies to direct their recruiting at the educated professionals who they also need so desperately."

Never one to criticize a program unless he can offer an alternative solution, Smith makes the following suggestion: "Instead of just one or two Bible or theological courses which are limited by academic requirements for admission there should be another parallel option. It would be designed for those who might never have even passed grade eight and are well beyond the years of acceptability to an admissions board. If they were permitted to take a limited instructional course and not be under the strain of meeting academic grades, many would probably apply and be willing to serve, if only for a short time. The area of their field work should be basic and would release skilled and qualified personnel for specialized work.

"It's not unlike what happened during the last war," he argues. "Men and women with limited education, who were not physically fit or were of advanced years, filled basic jobs. This released able-bodied men for the armed forces or vital defense work. Why couldn't missions have the same program?"

It is difficult to write off his theory when besides himself, Smith can list other religious leaders of note such as D. L. Moody, Gypsy Smith or P. W. Philpott, men who in some cases never even saw the inside of a school. These men, plus countless others, went on to leave a permanent mark in the Christian world.

At 8:00 P.M. on October 9th, he made the following entry in his diary.

"I have decided to take the long course, but oh it's so dark."

Having made the decision, Smith became an active, full-time student at Manitoba College. He entered into the student activities which also included the initiation ceremony. This harrowing experience included being dragged out of bed at midnight, bounced in a blanket as high as possible, tied to a beam in the college's basement by a dirty rope, and being daubed about the neck and face with dirty red paint. Following all this he was nearly drowned by icy cold water from a hose. The greatest indignity of all was being herded with the other freshmen before the arrogant sophomores and made to sing, play or recite upon command. It was all in fun but it wasn't funny to the performers.

Smith found the classes and subjects extremely difficult. He was now taking Greek, Latin, French and the full matriculation course. This was all new to him and his limited education was very evident. He found it practically impossible to cope with the lectures, let alone the homework and assignments. Despite this he earnestly studied, many times until well after midnight. He enjoyed the challenge and was determined to make creditable grades.

On October 31st he, along with his new-found friends, decided to break away from the routine and celebrate Halloween. Dressed in their nightshirts they paraded the streets of Winnipeg in noisy ranks. They made a point of visiting the homes of their professors. One professor who went on to win national recognition, was Ralph Connor, the author of the immortal Canadian classic, *Glengarry School Days*. He received the students warmly and joined in the fun.

It was the practice of the college to send its student theologues out into the field to gain experience. For Smith this was ideal. Some of his classmates were nervous and unsure. It was a complete reversal of the classroom. Smith more than held his own as he preached in such picturesque prairie communities as Rosenfelt, Plum Coulee, Salem and Ingleside.

By mid-December he had finished his first term and was

burning the midnight oil, cramming for exams. Despite his insecurity and lack of confidence he fared remarkably well, only failing Greek which he dropped in favor of botany.

By the time the examination results were posted Smith had made definite plans to return to Mount Albert and spend the Christmas holidays with his family. It had been a year and four months since he had been home. His parents, brothers and sisters were overjoyed to have him with them once more. Because of his travels and adventures he was quite a celebrity in the community. Once the initial greetings were over he spent most of his waking hours telling everyone what he had seen and where he had been. Places like Winnipeg, Jasper, Vancouver, Port Essington were as romantic and mystical as Timbuktu to his enthralled listeners.

One tale he repeated over and over again was the story of his 100-mile sternwheeler trip, up the Skeena River to the Copper River in the interior of British Columbia. He told his younger brothers and sisters how the sailors had to walk along the banks and pull the boat up the river against the strong current by ropes. His word pictures were so real that all they had to do was to close their eyes and they could hear the grunting of the men and feel the spray in their faces.

His homecoming was highlighted by being invited to take over Reverend D. G. Cameron's pulpit in the Mount Albert Presbyterian Church for a Sunday service. This was the first time his parents and family had ever heard him preach.

"I have said many times that I've never really experienced fright in the pulpit and that is true, with probably this one exception. I think anyone will agree that one's own family is his most severe critic. When I stood up to preach I looked into those faces staring up at me, for a moment all I wanted to do was bolt off the platform. My sermon topic was 'The Servant Redeemer' taken from Mark 10:45. Once I got into the message and from time-to-time saw my mother quietly smile or nod to father in agreement, I knew that I had succeeded in pleasing them."

This was quite a different Christmas from the one twelve months previous when all Smith had for company was a few Indians in the wilds of British Columbia.

Smith returned to Winnipeg, full of enthusiasm for the next term at college. His moderate success with the Christmas exams gave him the added encouragement he needed to finish the year, but the next six months didn't come up to his high expectations.

When discussing this phase of his life he said, "I'm sure that if I had heeded God's voice and returned to Toronto Bible College I would have been spared many heartaches and trials. Manitoba College was not what I'd typify as being the ideal Christian training ground. At least in 1910 it wasn't. I had gone there expecting a high degree of spirituality among the students and especially the faculty. What I found was indifference, coolness and in many cases downright opposition to everything I was looking for in the way of Christian growth. I hasten to point out that I was looking at the situation through the eyes of a young man both in years and Christian experience. I'm sure that if I were to relive those days now I'd evaluate the situation differently, but it was most discouraging and disappointing.

"Many of my fellow theologues swore, smoked, played cards, attended the theatre and dances. I'd always considered these things a sign of carnal living. The professors and administrative staff appeared to go back on their word many times when it came to granting speaking assignments in the various churches or supplying approved expenses. In all fairness to them I'm sure that there were reasons behind their actions of which I was not aware. It's similar to a president of a company issuing directives which are not popular with the employees. He may be forced to do it and cannot divulge the details behind the decision. I'm not trying to be overly charitable in this instance, rather giving the benefit of the doubt. One area which I took strong exception to, and still do for that matter, was the action of the admission board. In my case, I spent over $200 of hard earned money to come to Winnipeg and take what I was assured would be the special five-year course. Instead, I was arbitrarily shunted into the expanded nine-year course. I was not the only one. In certain cases, this experience, plus the shock of college life, was enough to cause some promising young men of God to chuck the whole thing and return home. They never realized their life's desire to become a minister. I thank God that He was able to sustain me and teach me the all important lesson of not looking to man but keeping my eyes on Him. It was a difficult experience, but a valuable one."

The lesson, so painfully learned, instilled in Smith the importance of honoring commitments no matter what personal sacrifices might be involved.

By June, he realized that as far as he was concerned, further studies at Manitoba College were useless. The year, however, was not a complete loss. As he receded from most of his classmates he drew closer to God. Fortunately he was able to make friends with a couple of other theologues who were of like mind. They also found college life incompatible with their deep-seated Christian principles and as a result each one strengthened the other. The other benefit derived was the invaluable experience gained in the small churches on the prairies.

"Years later as I became involved with teaching organizations such as the Canadian Bible Institute, I realized that there were problems far greater than any of the students ever appreciated. One thing I learned from Manitoba was the practicability of classroom lectures being combined with actual field experience. I've always looked back on those days, when I criss-crossed the Manitoba countryside by horse and buggy and horseback, as the most productive and beneficial of my early training. Despite my apparent disobedience to God's calling I still came out on top because every day I learned something different which was to stay with me for the rest of my ministry. God works in many ways to hone and refine those He has chosen to preach His Word, whether it be in a small country church or in spacious halls and tabernacles throughout the world."

It always amazes Smith when someone asks him if he ever thought he would be anything more than just an average minister. He never had any doubt as to what his role in life would be. In fact, he was so certain that his was not just an ordinary calling that he wrote the following in his diary on April 24, 1910.

I can scarcely doubt that God has a great work for me and that the future years will see me preaching the Gospel of Jesus Christ to thousands. My one great thought day and night is evangelistic work. The impression is growing by the day that this is to be my work. Even while I'm working at my studies my thoughts wander off and I see myself preaching to hundreds of people in evangelistic meetings.

It was a small advertisement which led him initially to the Toronto Bible College and it was a small booklet written by J. George Stuart which led him out of Manitoba College. Entitled "Talks About Soul Winning," it confirmed in Smith's mind the fact that God wanted him to move on. This time there was no reluctance or uncertainty.

On June 2nd he left Winnipeg and spent the following summer months in rural Manitoba ministering to the rag-tag settlers who dotted the scrub-filled countryside.

His center of operation was the settlement of Hollywood. Unlike its California namesake in the lush Santa Monica Mountains, Hollywood, Manitoba, consisted of just one house inhabited by the district postmaster. Scattered around Hollywood were homesteads which provided the settlers with, at the very most, a marginal existence. Those who stuck to it to carve sections of land out of the wilderness became the foundations upon which family fortunes were made in the world famous Manitoba wheat fields.

For Smith, Manitoba was just as barren and inhospitable as British Columbia. His days were filled with one adventure after another. If he wasn't trying to control a spooky horse during a prairie thunderstorm he was trying to find his way home in the pitch blackness of dead night.

On one occasion he was nearly responsible for the death of a young hunting companion. "It would seem that every time I got mixed up with guns I was either in personal danger like the duck hunting escapade or through no fault of mine the means of nearly killing someone. The time I nearly killed someone happened during a duck and prairie chicken hunting trip with my former roommate at Manitoba College. We were crawling through the long grass leading up to a small lake and I was pulling my gun along beside me when suddenly the trigger must have caught in a twig or something and the gun went off. The shot came within inches of a young lad who was with the hunting party. When I realized how close I had come to killing the boy I bowed my head and fervently thanked God that He intervened and kept me from taking a life."

Circuit-riding, hazardous though it may have been in those days, had its rewards. Many times Smith was received as if he were a direct messenger from God. If you had to live as some of those he visited it's easy to understand their joy at seeing someone at their door . . . anyone! It was not uncommon for him to arrive at a homestead which was forty miles from the railway station and the same distance or more from a doctor, post office or neighbor. There were no telephone or telegraph lines within miles and the only road through the bush was dotted with large stumps and underbrush. Even if the roads were passable they were of little use until the freeze-up because horses were scarce. The usual means of transportation was by Red River cart which was drawn by a yoke of plodding oxen. The houses were built of rough hewn logs settled on dirt floors. One room served the family. If you wanted privacy you crouched behind a well-patched blanket or quilt which was hung from the rafters. Water, if available, was of questionable purity. Smith found it safer to wait until it was well boiled before taking the chance of even the slightest sip.

Perhaps it was the isolation, but whatever it was, the local people were clannish to the point of bitterness, especially between themselves. Not unlike the experiences of a large family, grudges born years before were nurtured and fanned to life from time to time. Some of those times happened when Smith was desperately trying to arrange Sunday services or weekly prayer meetings. It was not uncommon for him to be told that no one would come because a neighbor, who was at odds with Smith's host, would openly boycott the meetings. This resulted in small congregations — so small, in fact that more than once, he preached to only two people. Usually if the count rose to more than ten he thanked God for a packed house. He was discouraged more often than he was encouraged, but instead of giving up the experience drove him to a closer personal relationship with God.

As Smith rode his horse from place to place he had plenty

of time to search his soul and seek God's will. He prayed over and over again for God's blessing and pleaded to be shown if there was any sin in his life which was displeasing. It came to him that he would have to give up his one worldly pleasure before complete surrender was assured. All his life he had been a voracious reader (the type who is often classified as reading everything including the backs of corn flake boxes). Mostly his literary interests centered around biographies of outstanding Christians such as: John Wesley, Martin Luther, D. L. Moody, Ira Sankey, C. H. Spurgeon or David Brainerd. One glaring departure from this standard, however, was mystery stories. He avidly followed the detective section in the Glasgow Weekly News. He had difficulty understanding how the reading of a harmless fiction story could be the means of God withholding His blessing, but nevertheless he felt he must give it up. When he finally gave in he realized a wonderful peace. There were difficult days ahead as he preached the Gospel to the hardened sodbusters of western Manitoba and this peace helped sustain him.

Once the matter of complete consecration was settled, he spent his days in the saddle and nights by his bed praying for guidance for the coming year. He realized that his work in and around Hollywood would be over by early October. Unless God wanted him to remain as resident preacher he must move on. Returning to Manitoba College was out of the question. He had no intention of spending another year in such an environment. He was quick to accept his need of further training. His Christian life had taken on new meaning as a result of the hours spent in prayer and he had no intention of placing it in jeopardy by being out of the will of God.

He kept remembering the time God spoke to him at Hartley Bay. It was something he couldn't put out of his mind. "The more I thought about it the more I was convinced that I'd made a terrible mistake. I should have heeded God's voice and gone directly to Toronto Bible College instead of wasting a year at Manitoba College. I was determined to make up for it and even decided on what I'd like to do if God opened up the way.

"First, I'd enroll in the day classes at Toronto Bible

College. Second I'd organize a Sunday school of 'Street Arabs' (poor children from the slums). Third, I'd get some consecrated young men and women to join with me and hold open air meetings as long as the weather permitted. When we would be driven off the streets we'd continue indoors holding mission services wherever possible.

"Once I'd confirmed the plans in my mind and prayed about them I felt quite satisfied and looked toward the coming year with expectation."

For the next three months until he boarded the train and headed for Winnipeg it was long hours in the saddle and longer nights in prayer. The experiences God permitted him to have shaped his compassion for missions and missionaries. He knew first hand what it was to be discouraged. He knew how it felt to knock on a door long after dark, the only door for miles, and not be certain of the welcome.

Everything has a purpose, especially for those called of God. For Smith, this was his time of trial and testing.

He left Winnipeg and headed for Fort William where he boarded the S.S. *Athabasca* and sailed across Lake Superior on his way to Toronto. He thought about all that had happened during the past twelve months and quietly rated the people he met and the sermons he preached as the high points. His sermon register shows that from October 31, 1909, when he preached on "The Servant Redeemer" in the Presbyterian Church in Ingleside, Manitoba, until October 2, 1910, when he addressed the congregation of the Presbyterian Church in Flora, Manitoba, on "The Seven Words From the Cross," he preached a total of 58 sermons. This figure does not include scores of prayer meetings, house calls or words of witness.

He once summed up those months by saying, "I'm firmly convinced that I was not where I should have been, but it proved one thing to me. God never wastes time or talent. He made me pay dearly for going against His will, but He rewarded me richly for everything I did. I'm positive that someday I shall meet many of those souls in Heaven. God's Word never dies regardless of who does the preaching. I've never regretted one moment I spent ministering on the prairies."

Chapter 7

Within a couple of days of arriving at Manitoba College Smith wrote in his diary, "Oh, the terrible, terrible darkness, confusion and agony now upon me."

Within a couple of days following his enrollment at Toronto Bible College a year later he wrote, "How pleasant it is to enter the old beloved school once more. It's thrilling to listen to the Word of God being expounded by such men as: Reverend John McNichol (Principal); Reverend William Stewart (President); Dr. Elmore Harris (Founder) and the teachers which include Andrew Imrie; T. Bradley Hyde and J. Griffith-Thomas (all ordained ministers)."

The joy of being a day student at T.B.C. was reflected in his progress. Instead of finding the lectures difficult he could hardly wait for classes to begin. Since everything studied centered around the Bible his interest and attention was complete. No longer did he have to struggle with languages, social sciences or advanced mathematics. He had finally found his rightful place.

In a matter of just a week or so he was well on his way to accomplishing two thirds of his prepared plan for the coming year. He had enrolled in Bible College and within a few days was finding it difficult to accept any further speaking engagements. His appointment book was filled.

His first and most memorable address was given in St. Andrew's Hall, the temporary home of St. Mark's Presbyterian Church. His minister, Reverend J. D. Morrow, opened up the pulpit to his enthusiastic young friend.

"It will be the first city church I have ever spoken in and it seems to me to be one step nearer to the work I long for," recorded Smith.

Perhaps it was the exposure to a city congregation that first started Smith to be critical of his platform manner. Until then he had merely jumped up in front of his audience and let go. There was little thought given to the strain he must have been placing on the ears of his listeners.

This critical evaluation of his platform technique and ability, in his diary, speaks for itself:

> I notice a great difference in my speaking lately. It has changed entirely from what it once was and keeps changing continually. My first preaching was loud and boisterous. It was also very fast and more often than not jerky. Now I have quieted down a great deal and speak with far more expression than ever before. I'm also much slower. I don't know how in the world people ever sat and listened to me. As I look back on different addresses I have given I can see many points which were in error. I sure made mistakes. I can now see a daily improvement. I watch my movements very closely and listen to my tone as I speak. I'm very conscious of what I'm saying and desperately trying to improve as quickly as possible. I love to have people criticize and point out my mistakes. I listen carefully to what they say and try to make sure I never am criticized for the same thing twice. I think I'm getting better. I pray that God will make me a great preacher some day.

Never one to pass up something which might be a benefit in later years Smith took advantage of the opportunity to study and practice dentistry. The ground rules under which he trained were not exactly in keeping with the high standards set for today's university students. An elderly dentist, Dr. W. A. Adams, had a standing offer that he would personally teach any Christian student the basic elements of dentistry. He felt that this was his contribution to the work of missions. There wasn't any question of these students becoming practicing dentists. It was only so that they would be able to minister to the natives once they reached the foreign field. Dr. Adams felt that even their limited knowledge would be better than nothing at all. Smith enjoyed the experience and quickly gained confidence. Under the close supervision of Dr. Adams he prepared, filled and extracted a number of teeth.

On November 3rd he was appointed to lead the College's missions study class on Africa every Saturday night. This completed his week as every free moment was just about filled. Everything in his life now centered around the college, the ministry and his Bible. He would have wanted it no other way.

The complete monopolization of his time had dramatic effects. He became impatient with the progress of his spiritual life. In fact, he has never really been satisfied with it at any time in his life. For a man with Smith's drives and passions this was to be expected. Instead of weakening his fervor for a closer walk with God it drove him to his knees. All extraneous interests and stimuli were shut out.

On November 4, 1910, he made the following dramatic entry in his diary:

> Reverend Andrew Imrie brought some great truths on living close to Christ in today's lecture. He highlighted prayer and devotion. I freely admit that I'm not in the place where God would have me be. I've not the love for souls I ought to have. I don't spend the time in Bible study and prayer I should. "Oh God, bend me to Thy will. Lead me into the inner circle, consecrate me fully, exclude selfishness, ambitions, make me humble. Shed abroad Thy love in my heart by the Holy Spirit. Oh Father, draw me near, give me souls. This is my cry."

By late November Smith had attracted enough interest that he was chosen, along with five other students to be one of the speakers at the Students' Public Meeting. This was the highlight of the fall term and to be chosen was deemed an outstanding honor.

The program was scheduled to begin at 8 P.M. on the night of November 28th, in the College's assembly hall on College Street. The building was directly across the street from the internationally famous Toronto General Hospital.

One of the other students speaking that night was Harry Bower, Smith's close friend. Bower graduated from the College and for many years leading up to his death was a city mission

73

worker. He made a significant contribution to the spiritual and material needs of the underprivileged through his work as Superintendent of Toronto's Sackville Street Mission.

He remembered the Students' Meeting vividly. "It was a great experience. Just to be picked was exciting and terrifying at the same time. Oswald and I were good friends. When it was announced that we were chosen we had serious doubts as to our ability even to open our mouths let alone present an address. The very thought of facing the critical student body in a formal meeting was unnerving. Neither of us minded speaking to strangers because we knew we probably wouldn't see many again. Our classmates were different. All you had to do was make a slight slip and you would hear about it for months. The best thing was to practice and get everything down pat. Oswald and I listened to each other over and over again. We criticized each other very pointedly. It helped because it gave each of us confidence. I know that Oswald memorized his complete address. I wondered at this because he had always said that all he ever did was memorize the sermon outline and fill out the address as he went along.

"Posters were printed and passed out. This was the first time that either Oswald or I, or any of the others participating, had been involved in a professionally promoted meeting. It was frightening to see our names listed. It was also gratifying to know that people, complete strangers, would be reading about the meeting and seeing our names in print as principal speakers.

"As we gained confidence in our ability and the evening drew near we turned more and more to the Lord in prayer. It was all that we had to sustain ourselves. Everything that could be done was done — it was out of our hands. I know that the other four felt the same way as we did.

"I was listed as the first speaker and my subject was 'The Work of the School.' Oswald was fifth and as you might expect his subject was missions, 'A Call to the Foreign Field.' The entire program went off without a hitch. It was a letter perfect evening. I listened to each address and could not fault any of them on content or presentation. Dr. Elmore Harris was the Chairman and following the meeting he congratulated each

74

one and said it was an honor being on the same platform. This was the lift that we needed — although secretly, Oswald told me he thought he did pretty well and I told him that I was well satisfied with my own performance.

"Following the meeting Oswald said he got a shock when he saw his father and aunt, Mrs. Thomas Findley. He said that he never even noticed them in the audience. He was grateful to God that he didn't because he said it would have made him more nervous than he already was."

Almost anyone who keeps a diary falls into the trap of starting off numerous entries with something like, "the most eventful experience in my life took place today," or "today was the most exciting of my life." Smith is no different. Generally speaking such entries are honest because they are written in the light of immediacy.

One experience really was "the most eventful moment of his life . . ." up to that point.

"Ever since I'd gone forward in Massey Hall I'd had a desire to be an evangelist and that desire drove me to concentrate all my efforts with that in mind," Smith recalled. "I sincerely believed that this was God's plan for my life. It could be considered presumptuous for me to say so but I honestly thought I had above average ability for an evangelistic ministry. I thought that for those with less qualifications, the foreign fields offered an avenue of service. It boiled down to, 'Keep the good ones at home and send the rest out as missionaries.' I was never one to back myself into a corner without an alternative so I reasoned that if God opened up the way for me as an evangelist I'd follow that path. If on the other hand He didn't I could always become a missionary. I soon learned once again that God's way is not always my way."

Duncan E. McDonald, who went to India as a Presbyterian missionary following graduation, became the catalyst who brought to Smith the vision of his irrevocable goal in life.

"Duncan asked me to speak on 'The Need of the Non-Christian World.' As I began to prepare for the message I suddenly realized that it would be absolute hypocrisy for me to stand up and tell my fellow students what my views were on the needs of the non-Christian world when I couldn't back them up. How, I wondered, could I ask someone to work for and support something I was not fully behind myself?

"Deeply troubled by this I took Duncan aside and told him that I just couldn't speak on such a subject because I was more interested in evangelism than I was in missions. He asked me if perhaps it wasn't a selfish interest? I had to admit it was."

Following his talk with McDonald he heard a message by a visiting speaker entitled "The Kingdom's Advance in the Orient." At the close of the meeting he had a private talk with the speaker, a Mr. H. W. Robins. During the conversation Robins looked at him intently and said, "If your desire to be an evangelist is to win men and women to Christ, and nothing more, then there is no reason why you can't be an evangelist in the foreign fields. If, on the other hand, your desire is based on speaking to large crowds it doesn't amount to very much."

He really hit close to home. This was what Smith had feared to admit or hear.

"I had always tried to excuse myself by saying that my whole desire was to win men and women to Christ . . . it wasn't. There was a selfish motive behind it. For the first time I was openly admitting it to myself that all I wanted was to become famous as a great evangelist. It was the one thing in my life that was holding me back.

"Thank God, I was able to receive the answer clearly and unmistakably. I was to go where the need was the greatest without consideration of personal preferences.

"I remember the day. It was Tuesday, December 8, 1910, that I wrote in my diary, 'The great struggle is over, I surrendered completely to God. I now trust that He will send me out to the foreign field. I do not care if my life is hidden away, unknown by the civilized world, as long as it is known to Him.'"

This marked the beginning of a career which has resulted in Oswald Smith, some 60 years later, being called "Canada's Elder Missionary Statesman."

Regardless of the year, January is usually the coldest, snowiest and most disagreeable month of winter. There are the occasional exceptions in Toronto . . . January, 1911, was not one of them.

Christmas and New Year's were over and a general apathy had settled in. Most people tried to recover from the celebrations both physically and financially as quietly as possible.

Smith decided that this was the right time to launch an evangelistic campaign. The fact that no one else seemed to share his views didn't deter his enthusiasm. Once he decided to proceed there were two major hurdles to face. First, he had to secure an auditorium and second he had to fill it or at least attract some semblance of an audience.

He had originally thought of holding the services in the old St. Mark's Presbyterian Church, but that was out because it was now being used as a factory. For a while he was stumped. Either the building or church he considered wouldn't suit him — or he didn't suit them. Remembering one of his earlier meetings in the Missionary Tabernacle on Bathurst Street he took a chance and called the minister.

"It took a lot of nerve to call Reverend A. W. Roffe because I was just a voice on the phone to him. After I outlined what I had in mind he asked for a few days to consider it. Those three days seemed like an eternity until he returned my call. He gave me permission to go ahead and hold my campaign in his church. I realize now what a chance he was taking."

This was to be Smith's first experience at a full-scale promotion. For a youth in his early twenties, he approached it quite professionally.

Publicity was the first item on the agenda and 3,000 posters were prepared. At one of Smith's earlier meetings there was an outstanding response to his message and seventeen boys stepped forward to make their decision. He called upon as many of these new converts as he could round up and had them, along with other volunteers, distribute the posters door-to-door in the area surrounding the church.

Once the meetings were announced and interest shown Smith received offers of assistance from J. D. Morrow and Mr. Roffe. Realizing how valuable these experienced men could be to the success of the crusade he accepted their offer with gratitude. The fact that they were interested and even offered to help gave him an added lift.

The program was basic. He would preach at each service which would be filled out with congregational singing and special musical numbers. After much prayer he decided on his sermons and they were announced as follows:

Monday . . . "The Love of God"
Tuesday . . . "Seeing Jesus"
Wednesday . . . "The Supreme Choice"
Thursday . . . "The Lost Opportunity"
Friday . . . "An Honest Seeker"

While not spectacular, the response to his preaching was encouraging. Five people went forward to accept Christ. They included a man and wife, a young girl, a business woman and a soldier.

The other intangible side-benefit was the opportunity to meet Jennie Tyrrell who was the guest soloist on Friday night.

Miss Tyrrell graduated from T.B.C. in 1909 and at the time of the crusade was training for the foreign field at the Nursing At Home Mission.

Smith in Stanley Park, Vancouver, B. C., 1908

Chapter 8

Billy Graham Crusades have become the hallmark for modern twentieth century evangelism. To propogate his modern version of religious fundamentalism Graham employs big business techniques. He readily admits that he uses "the best technical aids to bring man within the sound and sight of the Gospel." No one, not even his severest critics, can question the effectiveness of this approach. All anyone has to do to be convinced is attend his meetings and see the packed auditoriums and stadiums with the streams of people coming forward under conviction. The evangelist, who was singled out by one public opinion poll, as the fourth most admired man in the United States, ranking only behind Mr. Eisenhower, Mr. Johnson and Senator Edward Kennedy, makes no apology for his techniques.

Nearly sixty years ago, the only public address system was a megaphone or strong pair of lungs. Closed circuit television had its counterpart in an overflow room where the audience strained to see and hear what was going on in the main auditorium through an open door.

It was during this period that John Wilbur Chapman and Charles McCallon Alexander held their now famous city-wide crusade in Toronto's Massey Hall.

Alexander was the same man who five years earlier had teamed up with R. A. Torrey in the evangelistic meetings which resulted in the conversion of Oswald Smith and his brother.

Chapman and Alexander's techniques were so close to being an early edition of the Graham Crusades that one might think Graham and his team copied from the success of their predecessors.

Smith remembers the meetings clearly because he was active as an usher and personal worker. "Chapman and Alexander had a large team of evangelists working with them. This meant that they would cover the whole city at the same time. The city was divided into twelve centers where nightly meetings were held by the various preachers. Each man had his own soloist who usually doubled as song leader. This was a good idea because music was very important and it helped keep the program at a high level. One of the soloists was the son of Gypsy Smith.

"The main meetings were held in Massey Hall by Chapman and Alexander. They were the climax of the regional meetings and warranted the build-up. Chapman was an excellent preacher with all the qualities that mark greatness. His sermon presentations were strong, earnest, solemn, forceful and touching. Alexander hadn't diminished in ability either. He was still the greatest song leader I've ever heard or seen in action on a public platform. The only one to compare with him is Cliff Barrows. Robert Harkness was at the piano and the crusade soloist was a man called Naftzger. I can't remember his first name or much about him.

"Backing up the platform party were scores of ushers and personal workers. Is it any wonder that they are often compared with Graham?"

Smith was in his element. Night after night he would serve as usher and then remain long after the benediction counseling those who came forward. It took the experienced skill of the senior personal worker to open his eyes and show him exactly how to lead a soul to Christ.

"Once again all I can remember is the man's last name. It was Norton. I might have forgotten his full name but I'll never forget how he operated. It was magnificent.

"It happened on the last night of the campaign. I was at my post in Massey Hall and had just spoken to a man about salvation. When he told me he was a Christian I moved on

80

looking for someone else to approach. I noticed a man about thirty years of age but didn't speak to him because he looked like a Christian. Just then, Mr. Norton appeared and went right up to the man. Since I was only a couple of feet away I could hear practically every word. Norton began witnessing and in less than five minutes he had led that man to Christ. I'll never forget it. I had just received my greatest lesson in soul-winning."

Smith freely admits that up to that time he had always taken much longer to deal with someone. It bothered him that he could never really be sure whether or not the decision was clear-cut. There was always a lingering doubt in his mind. Norton proved to him that time is relative when it comes to personal work. He saw that it was possible to lead someone to Christ, without a shadow of doubt, in just a few minutes.

The next diary entry reflected his great admiration for Norton, his ability and obvious close communion with God.

"Give me that power which will lead souls to Thee," he wrote. "Oh that I had it! Every time I preach the Gospel and give an invitation I want to see souls saved. Lord, I pray that especially in personal work, the hardest of all Christian work, that I may be brought to the place where my life will be so in harmony with God's that it will be completely consecrated and surrendered. I pray that the Holy Spirit will so fill me that when I speak to a lost soul about Jesus it may result in a definite acceptance of Christ as his personal Saviour, Lord and King. May God be able to so perfectly control my life in prayer, that my testimony may be a power irresistible to winning souls."

The meetings, while stimulating spiritually, were also memorable for a far different reason. A deep personal relationship was budding between Smith and Jennie Tyrrell. Up to this point in his diary of personal remembrances, there is no mention of a romantic involvement. This is not to imply that as an adolescent, he was oblivious to girls. Rather he was so completely involved and dedicated to his Christian life that they did not enter into his world . . . until Jennie Tyrrell.

What had begun as a mere acquaintance at the Missionary

Tabernacle Meetings blossomed into a serious relationship which evolved into a two-year engagement.

In describing Jennie Tyrrell in his diary Smith didn't dwell on the physical — instead his entries highlight the aesthetic.

On January 31, 1911, he wrote, "She is the most beautiful Christian I've ever met."

On May 8th he elaborated further. "I have never met a more nobler, more pure minded Christian woman.

"She has helped me greatly and I've enjoyed her friendship. We have worked together in meetings and her dedication is complete. She has volunteered for the foreign field as a missionary. I hope she realizes her desire."

Their engagement was marked by a series of upheavals which undoubtedly resulted from the strong spiritual relationship each one had with the Lord. The problem centered around each one's conception of what being in the will of God involved. Unlike many first-time romances this one didn't end in bitterness. Instead, it terminated in a mutual understanding. They, especially Smith, realized painfully, that because of their deep-rooted dedication it would be best if they went their separate ways rather than have their lives working at cross-purposes.

The engagement was broken on March 25, 1914, when Jennie Tyrrell returned her engagement ring. This wrote "Finished" to one of Smith's most moving, personal involvements. His innermost thoughts were summed up in the last stanza of "Sorrow's Benediction," the poem he wrote about that unhappy day.

> Darkness and gloom beyond my comprehension
> Until I knelt submissive to His will;
> Now all is light, ineffable in brightness —
> O wondrous love, beyond my knowledge still!

During the years of the engagement Smith's professional career matured as he moved about North America gaining experience.

His grades at the completion of his first full year at Toronto Bible College were excellent. It must be pointed out that he was taking subjects in which he was deeply interested. Nevertheless, the marks were far above average, in fact they were among the best in his class:

Ephesians	93%
Old Testament	92%
Psalms	90%
Homiletics	93%
Doctrines	95%
History	91%
Missions	89%

During these years his career took many and varied twists. Each one resulted in the gaining of valuable experience which fitted him well for the role he was to begin playing. He would shortly see his ministry and influence break out of provincial bounds and take on international scope.

Following the Chapman-Alexander Crusade he accepted an invitation from the Pocket Testament League of Canada to become their first traveling secretary. While the range of his operation was not extensive, he became well known in the more populated areas of Ontario. His addresses in the churches of Galt, Preston, Guelph, Waterloo, Kitchener, and Woodstock were covered by the local press. This was his first exposure to being quoted publicly. It was quite exciting on August 15th, 1911, when he read the following report in the Woodstock *Sentinel Review*.

> Mr. Smith stated that the Pocket Testament League is a worldwide undenominational organization of those who agree to read a chapter of the Bible daily.
> He emphasized the fact that the Bible was the greatest of all books and made a powerful plea for it to be made the constant companion of every one who honored Christ's name.
> Mr. Smith is an attractive speaker with a clear voice and strong personality.

His most cherished memento from that period is a letter he received from Fanny J. Crosby, the internationally famous blind hymn writer.

P.O. Box 840
Bridgeport, Connecticut
May 8, 1911

Mr. Oswald J. Smith
Toronto Ontario
Canada

Dear Brother:

When I go to address audiences it is my custom to carry in my hand my Little Pocket Testament which seems to inspire me and give me confidence that the great author of its lines is near me. Then, in quiet hours at home, as I sit in my room composing, I still hold my testament close in my hand.

Sincerely yours,
Fanny J. Crosby

It was also during this two-year period that Smith became the full-time minister of the Belwood Congregational Church. Belwood is a small hamlet about 80 miles north-west of Toronto. The closest community of any significance is the town of Fergus. Coupled with the Belwood charge was another appointment, two miles away, with the quaint sounding name of Garafraxa, Ontario.

Reverend John McNichol, the Principal of T.B.C., sent Smith to Belwood for what was to be a Sunday engagement. The congregation liked the tall, intense preacher so well that they asked him back, again and again. What had begun as a simple supply ministry ended in a call. The pulpit committee did their utmost to convince Smith that Belwood and Garafraxa needed him as their minister. They even went so far as to offer the same salary they were prepared to pay an ordained minister . . . $7.00 a week, clear!

"I liked the congregations and they liked me. It was a wonderful time. I preached my first sermon at Belwood on November 22, 1911. My subject was 'The Need of the Non-Christian World.' I concluded my ministry on September 1, 1912. I'll always remember those last two services. I spoke on 'The Life Beyond the Grave.' It was a moving experience. I knew that I'd probably never see many of them again and I suppose they realized it also. There was an air of genuine love in those tiny churches. I often think that it is impossible to duplicate such an atmosphere in a large church. You really need to be close to your congregation and they to you, to feel that surge of love. It's a rare experience, I thank God that I was able to enjoy it, if only for a brief time."

While he was serving the Belwood and Garafraxa churches

he was also attending T.B.C. His grades maintained the high standard he had set the previous year. His overall average was a creditable 86.3%. His academic achievements and spiritual contributions to the life of the College, earned him the singular honor of being named class valedictorian.

On April 26, 1912, he wrote, ". . . the building was filled, this included the side rooms and gallery. Fred Vine spoke first, then Etta Cole. I followed with the valedictory address. After the people had gone we held a prayer meeting which lasted until nearly twelve o'clock. It was a most gracious time. . . . Mother came from Mount Albert for the graduating exercises."

Graduating from any institution, regardless of whether it be high school, college or university, can be a traumatic experience. The graduate is suddenly thrust out of a familiar environment into a hostile society. No matter how definite his plans and hopes are, he is usually wracked by insecurity and doubts. Smith was no different.

Fortunately, he had given serious consideration about the direction he wanted his life to take following T.B.C. Two possibilities were open: Livingstone's Medical College in England or McCormick Theological Seminary of Chicago. Either would, if he were successful, provide a firm grounding for his future ministry.

As had been his pattern in the past, he spent long days and nights praying for guidance. The longer he prayed the more he thought about McCormick. Deciding that this was his answer he applied for admittance and was accepted. Admission to McCormick had one major attraction. Besides being a highly respected institution it was the seminary of the Presbyterian Church of America and Smith wanted the recognition and prestige accorded one of its alumni.

He was now nearing his mid-twenties and knew that his student days were drawing to an end. It was time that he began making a serious contribution to the work of the Lord. He had reached a point in life where, had he chosen the business world, he would probably have had ten years of work and experience behind him. Many of his boyhood chums who had left school between the ages of 13 and 16 were now firmly established and raising a family. Smith was still a student.

Smith had never before seen anything like Chicago. Toronto had earned the title of "Toronto the Good" with a church on every corner. Chicago was wide open. Instead of a church on every corner there was either a bar, flop-house, betting parlor or bordello. Prohibition was just a few years away. Al Capone, Dutch Schultz, and the other gang lords had not yet made their impact on the "crime" center of the nation. The foundations however, were well-laid for an eventual take-over and the reign of terror which followed.

Right in the midst of the crime and corruption in down town Chicago was the world-famous Moody Church. It became Smith's point of spiritual contact.

The importance of finding Moody and being able to attend filled a large vacuum in his life. He was, at that time, still emotionally involved with Jennie Tyrrell. The long-distance romance took its toll. Coupled with this was the restlessness of not being completely involved.

On September 23, 1912, he wrote, "I find that the hardest thing for me to do here is to have patience. I long to be in active work and it is most difficult for me to settle down to three years of quiet study. Much as I enjoy college life here at McCormick this problem is difficult to accept, much less overcome."

With only classes at McCormick and services at Moody to take up his time, Smith turned to reading. It didn't matter whether it was the Bible during morning devotions, or a manual on street corner soul winning, he had the knack of being able to become completely absorbed and withdraw from the outside world.

"I had always been fascinated by biographies of outstanding preachers and evangelists. Up to this point in my reading the one which impressed me most was the deeply personal autobiography of Charles G. Finney. I had read and reread this book during my ministry in Hollywood, Manitoba. It was

86

this book which gave me my burden for revival and the fullness of the Spirit.

"While at McCormick, I had plenty of spare time on my hands. I began reading 'Brainerd's Journal' during that period of intense loneliness. I was completely captivated by the life of this outstanding Christian who was called 'The Man of Prayer.'

"I started reading the book around the middle of November and on the 20th I wrote in my diary, 'I have never read or heard of any man who died more to self and labored so fully for God's glory.'

"He was a missionary to the American Indians in the mid-1700's and only lived to the age of twenty-nine . . . but what a life! Perhaps it was because I was his contemporary in years that I identified so closely with him. Whatever it was, I've never lost the vision of Brainerd and when I'm asked who influenced my life most I have to say without hesitation, Finney and Brainerd."

By early December Smith was in dire financial straits. His ministry at Bellwood was significantly more rewarding spiritually than financially. He had arrived in Chicago three months earlier with around $100.00 and no promise of any more. Asking his parents for assistance was out of the question because his father had all he could do to maintain a liveable existence for a growing family still at home. Smith did receive a gift at Christmas which touched him deeply because he realized the sacrifice his parents had made on his behalf.

On December 9th he was down to 95¢ and deeply in debt to another student and the college. It would have been impossible to continue had it not been for the college aid he received. It amounted to $21.00 each month — after deductions for in-residence living expenses were made. By the time each payment was received, Smith usually had to resolve his outstanding debts and start over again, trying to exist for another month. To cut down he eliminated one meal a day and grew accustomed to such a routine. Since he was not speaking regularly he missed the additional income no matter how small. All he had left was prayer and on the 9th he turned everything over to God taking as his promise, Philippians 4:19 — "And my God will supply every need of yours according to his riches in glory in Christ Jesus."

His answer was not immediate, in fact it didn't come until he had put in two more months of marginal living.

On February 9, 1913, he was sent by Reverend George L. Robinson, one of his professors, to supply the pulpit of the Millard Avenue Presbyterian Church in Southwest Chicago. They needed an interim minister and were willing to pay a salary of $10.00 per week.

February was a good month for Smith. Coupled with the call to Millard Presbyterian and the financial security it offered, was the psychological up-lift of seeing his writings in print. His first published poem, "The Call of the Orient," appeared in the *Herald Presbyter*. The magazine also rated his work sufficiently to publish a second piece, "The Dawning of the Light."

The poem was five stanzas in length. One only has to know a little about Smith's life and ambitions to realize that he was pouring out his heart when he wrote:

> Teach me to say, O Master Divine,
> "Thy will be done, my Father, not mine."
> Thou hast a purpose hidden from me,
> Oh may I trust and leave all with Thee.

February was also report month. This was the crucial period, the point of no return, for many students. Those who failed, or were borderline cases, were usually asked to withdraw and try again next term. This would have been completely unacceptable to Smith. He applied himself diligently. The results reflected his intense application:

English Bible	"A"
History of Missions	"A"
Music	"A"
Church History	"B"
Philosophy	"B"
Apologetics	"C"
Homiletics	"C"
Religious Biography	"C"

Only five in the class of over fifty received an "A" in English Bible. Most of these had already received their Bachelor of Arts Degrees.

On May 4, 1913, he closed his ministry at Millard Presbyterian. During those months twelve responded to his preaching and made definite decisions.

Two days later on the 6th he left for Harlan in the hills of Kentucky. He had read many of John Fox, Jr's., books that year and had been stimulated by the stories of the mountaineers. This is where he wanted to spend the summer in the service of the Lord.

As he stepped off the train in Harlan, and rode through the Cumberland Mountains on horseback, he was in effect riding into another world. The people were different, as different as their customs. They were a race apart. The mountaineers made their own rules and were a law unto themselves. Anyone familiar with the history of the Internal Revenue Department in the United States is well aware of the constant battle between the government and the moonshiners. Strangers were resented. If one did manage to break into the tightly knit community, family feuds were often stopped long enough for the interloper to be dealt with in convincing and decisive style.

Smith had confirmed his summer's work by writing letters and making the necessary contacts before he left Chicago. Ambitious as he was to serve in the hills of Kentucky, he was not naive enough to arrive in the area unannounced or unexpected. His offer was quickly accepted. He was assigned to a field of service which had Cawood, a small hamlet consisting of a combined store-post office and one house, as his home base.

His diary is filled with descriptions of the area and its people. Despite their weakness for corn liquor, family feuds, lazy days in the shade and a foul smelling tobacco called shag, they were basically warm, God-fearing people.

Smith's mother was always remembered by her family for "setting the best table in Ontario." She was an excellent cook and prided herself on mastering most of the good Canadian

89

dishes such as roast beef or chicken. Her stews would tempt a king and on special occasions, such as Christmas or Thanksgiving, she had the "finest tom turkey in the country" with all the fixings.

Brought up on such delicacies, Smith was in for a rude awakening when he sat down to his first Kentucky hillbilly dinner.

"We sat down at eleven instead of twelve because the mountain folk rise at four or five in the morning and go to bed by seven. It was the strangest meal I've ever eaten.

"There were several men and boys present. We all sat down together with the women and young girls scurrying about the room as they waited on the table which was covered with a well-worn oil cloth. It was the first time I was to eat their hot corn bread. I didn't know what to do so watched the other men. As the plate was passed each one broke off a large chunk with his fingers. I did the same when my turn came. The corn bread was quite flat and looked much like what we in Canada call Johnny cake. It was cooked in grease and the housewife told me that 'it jest don't taste right any other way.'

"The table was well-laid with platters of fat pork, squirrel, chicken, rabbit and fish which were also cooked in grease and dripped as you lifted a serving onto your plate. Even the potatoes were fried in grease. There was only one vegetable served and it usually was potatoes. I found out later that they don't like anything dry. That is one statement I never questioned.

"We only had one dish to eat from, a large dinner plate. When I had finished my main course I scraped off as much grease as I could with my corn bread and spooned out the dessert, which was apple sauce and honey. To wash everything down I had a choice of coffee or sour milk. They never used tea and before I left the area I often longed for a good cup of tea like my mother used to make.

"It was a strange gathering around the table, unlike anything I had ever experienced before. Meals were for eating, not socializing. There was little or no table conversation. Once the meal was finished the men kicked their chairs back and bolted for the door."

Smith lived alone in the manse beside the church which was half a mile down the road from the combination post office and store.

During the next few months he spent most of his time roaming over the mountain trails on the back of a stubborn mule, preaching and ministering to his scattered congregation. Generally he was received with warm enthusiasm. It was a lonely ministry. Out of these experiences came some of his finest poems which set the tone for much of his writings in later years.

Al Capp, the cartoonist, created Li'l Abner and Dogpatch to amuse the comic page readers. Smith could have given him many story-board outlines which he could have used for his mystical characters. One was a harrowing experience which took place during the evening of July 13th, which could have resulted in serious injury or even death.

The area over the mountain had the reputation of being the toughest, roughest, hard-drinkingest community around. Smith and Bernard Burkhart, a Christian mountaineer, decided to hold a series of evangelistic meetings for the people in the area. They were given permission to use a nearby schoolhouse and began preaching the Gospel. Attendance was good right from the first service. Encouraged by the response, Smith and his companion began praying for definite decisions, or at the very least, a renewed interest in the things of God.

Following one evening meeting shots rang out as the congregation left the schoolhouse. One bullet passed between a mule's legs and frightened the woman rider half to death. Another shattered a lantern which a man was holding to see what was happening. Another missed a man sitting on a veranda and buried itself in the logs above his head. Fortunately no one was hit.

Smith and Burkhart stood their ground and continued the meetings. On Friday night they announced that the services would resume the next Monday.

As Smith was saddling his mule on Monday he received a visit from one of the local women. She told him he'd be wise to forget about going back over the mountain, because a gang of local toughs was planning to waylay him on the trail and "do him up good." Evidently they didn't appreciate anyone with the Gospel upsetting their profitable moonshining operations. Their plans were well laid. The men had carefully picked out a spot on the trail for the ambush. They were even going to blacken their faces so as to be less conspicious as they laid in wait. Smith believed the woman because she told him that some of her own relatives were involved. As a result she broke the strongest code of the hills . . . informing on kin.

Smith was terrified. His first reaction was either to leave the area once and for all or at the very least cancel the meetings. His decision to carry on was not one of bravado, rather one of complete dependence upon God for His protection and strength. Wisely, he asked the superintendent of the Cawood Sunday school to go with him. Quietly as they could, they guided their mules along the trail which led to the schoolhouse. As they rounded a curve half-way down the mountain they spotted two of the gang coming after them. They were too far ahead to be caught and made the schoolhouse in safety. The return journey to Cawood was uneventful except for passing the two scowling roughnecks. No attempt was made to interfere because another friend of Smith's had joined the party and the two were outnumbered.

By mid-August Smith was in the depths of despair. This was partly due to the loneliness and isolation of his mission field and partly due to the cooling relationship between himself and Jennie Tyrrell. Their engagement had just a few months to run and Smith was being wracked by disappointment and uncertainties following each letter from his fiancee.

The highlight of his summer's work climaxed in a little place called Turtle Creek. Without this evidence of God's blessing Smith would quite probably have written off the entire effort as a waste of time.

The entries in his diary reflect the increasing enthusiasm and buoyed-up spirits which surfaced at this time. For many weeks the entries mainly concerned his loneliness, fits of depression, unrequited love, poor health and pleading for a touch from God.

Following August 20th, the tone was ecstatic as he summed up the meetings.

"These are the finest days of my ministry in Kentucky. Revival has taken place! I thank God that I was allowed to have a part in this wonderful manifestation of His power.

"The building was filled for each service with many standing along the walls. Everyone seemed interested and I could feel the Spirit of God as I preached. I gave the invitation each night and they came forward until the final count was forty-one. It is all the more remarkable because as far as I've been able to find out there is only one person in Turtle Creek who makes a definite profession of being a Christian.

"The interest has been so great that afternoon converts' meetings were organized. All types are accepting Christ. There are children, boys and girls, men and women, and even complete families. I can hardly believe what is happening. This has renewed my dedication to the Lord. I'll go on from this day confident in the power of God to save men from their sins."

Smith is convinced that the prelude to the Turtle Creek revival had begun two months earlier. At that time, he was just as depressed and weighed down as the atmosphere. The heat was oppressive and the humidity smothering. He was so discouraged that particular Sunday, that he wasn't even going to bother giving an invitation. As far as he was concerned it would be a complete waste of time. Somehow, he was led to give an invitation, which was half-hearted to say the least. To his surprise, four came forward. This was the first breakthrough. From then on Smith renewed his efforts to reach those pathetic mountain people, who had been all but written off by the outside world.

For the next few weeks until September 17th, when he left Cawood for Chicago and another year at McCormick Seminary, his spirits and outlook had taken a decided upswing. There was no repeat of the harassment from the rowdy element. His problems came from such unexpected areas as a balky horse and runaway mule. The horse threw him and he was lucky to escape with just a badly bruised hip and legs. The mule scared him nearly half to death, as it spooked and raced headlong down the trail. It was following these events that he wrote his poem, "The Voices."

His enthusiasm for McCormick coupled with a renewed tranquillity as he drew closer to the Lord, inspired him to compose a three-fold dedication to God. It was signed on the night of October 5, 1913 as he knelt by his bed.

1) I will think no thought, speak no word, and do no deed unworthy of a follower of Jesus Christ
2) I will give my life for service in any part of the world and in any capacity God wills that I should labor
3) I shall endeavour to do God's will from moment to moment as He reveals it to me.

Almost as if in answer to this complete dedication, he was called to be the pastor of the South Chicago Presbyterian Church at the magnificent salary of $60.00 per month. They also granted him full latitude in his duties, which meant that he could combine his pastoral responsibilities and academic demands admirably.

Everything was fitting into his plans. More important, he was sure that it was God's plan as well for his life. The next nine months of his life were months of complete fulfillment. The work at Chicago Presbyterian exceeded his wildest hopes and by January 8, 1914, he had mapped out a definite list of requirements for his church which he placed before God in prayer. The following is what he wanted for his pastorate.

1) to reach the unsaved for Christ
2) to turn Christians from worldliness to spirituality
3) to make the prayer meeting a live service
4) to build a large, enthusiastic Sunday school
5) to develop a strong missionary church
6) to increase church attendance
7) to put spiritual men in every office.

These aims are still valid nearly sixty years later. He has not changed one of them.

Smith began writing verse in 1906 and this talent was being recognized. On September 5, 1914, he had the aesthetic pleasure which comes to every creative individual, of seeing his work before the public. His first collection of hymns was published with music by Dr. D. B. Towner. Three days after this he completed what is probably his most introspective hymn and one which appears in many contemporary hymn-books.

"Deeper and Deeper" began as a melody which Smith formulated three years before while waiting to preach a sermon in Woodstock, Ontario. Many times during the intervening months he attempted to compose the words, but somehow they never quite worked out to his complete satisfaction. The metre was difficult and this held him back. After many days of concentration he finally wrote five verses. Each one is deeply moving and many consider this to be one of the finest examples of his skill as a hymnist.

In the five verses he portrays five steps in the Christian life: the heart; the will; the cross; joy and love. It is the last verse, however, which transports the soul to heights sublime:

> Into the love of Jesus
>> Deeper and deeper I go,
> Praising the One who brought me
>> Out of my sin and woe;
> And through eternal ages
>> Gratefully I shall sing,
> O how He loved! O how He loved!
>> Jesus, my Lord and my King.

By the time he reached his twenty-fifth birthday he had achieved far greater things than just living for a quarter of a century. He had become a man in every sense of the word. With this maturity came a settling of ambition. Gone was the uncertainty of youth and adolescence. In its place, there was conviction and an unshakeable optimism for the future. Being a creative individual, with definite ability in the field of writing, understandably he recorded his thoughts in an orderly manner. On his birthday November 8th he wrote the following in his diary:

"For seven years I have had the privilege of preaching the Gospel. I have asked God to direct me very definitely as to my life's work and am praying that He will make me:

1) a victorious man
2) a Spirit-filled man

3) a man of prayer
4) a man of the Word
5) a surrendered man
6) a man of one purpose."

When he arrived in Chicago three years earlier it was with a definite plan. He wanted to graduate from McCormick Seminary and be recognized by the Presbyterian Church.

On April 29th he was a member of the processional in the Graduating Class of 1915 and on the following night he was ordained by the Presbytery as a Presbyterian minister. The ordination service took place in the South Chicago Presbyterian Church which he was leaving for an assistant pastorate at Dale Presbyterian in Toronto. South Chicago pleaded with him to consider and become their permanent pastor. He was tempted but felt that he was definitely led of God to accept Reverend J. D. Morrow's invitation.

His life had now come full-cycle and, as he began his work at Dale, on Sunday, June 6th, he knew that rather than closing a chapter of his life he was really just beginning. The years of hardship, disappointment and struggle were eminently worthwhile. He was now a respected member of the clergy . . . more important he was a child of God, basking in the knowledge that he was in the will of his Master.

Dale Presbyterian Church

Chapter 9

John D. Morrow was a newspaperman's dream . . . he was good copy.

In a day when the papers were filled with stories of the war in Europe it took a good promoter, with an eye for what was really "news," to get his story on the front pages. John Morrow was just such a man.

He had a dream which became a reality. It was Dale Presbyterian Church, the finest new church in Toronto.

It took him seven years to build Dale at a cost of over $100,000. These were the years leading up to, and including, the beginning of World War I, when money and energies were being devoted to defeating "the Hun."

Morrow had a number of things going for him. Besides a striking personality, which he used to great effect, he was an athletic hero. Up to 1915 he held the Canadian record for quarter mile of 49⅘ seconds. He also ran the 100 yards in 10 seconds and the 220 in 22 seconds. He was a supreme opportunist and made the most of his athletic prowess. He was so successful that Dale was referred to as "The Athlete's Church" probably as often as it was by its own name.

Morrow was not above the dramatic gesture if it meant achieving his goal. Desperate for funds to continue the building of the church, he took to the street corners of downtown Toronto preaching and singing. He borrowed a "Pay As You Enter" box from the street car company and stood for hours begging donations for his building program.

On another occasion, when it looked as if the basement

of his church would remain uncompleted unless $2,500.00 was raised, he told his wife that he wasn't going to eat any solid food until the necessary funds were secured. For ten days he existed on nothing except water, despite the concerned pleas of his wife. He was a firm believer in the uselessness of suffering, no matter how worthwhile the cause, unless recognition was received. This time it paid off. A local financier, Sir John Gibson, took a liking to the brash preacher and agreed to underwrite a note at the bank. His faith in Morrow was justified. Within three months, the note was redeemed and there was a thousand dollars left over. The basement was completed and services began in "the roofless church."

The fact that his church was without a roof and uncompleted grated on Morrow. He suddenly announced that he would refuse to cut his hair or wear a hat as long as his church was open to the skies. Going without a hat in Toronto, especially in winter, was completely unheard of in those days. Much to the consternation of the local haberdashers, the practice began to catch on as his "gimmick" was played up in the local press. He had, without intending to do so, become a trendsetter in male attire.

Morrow became a colorful figure on the streets of downtown Toronto. His lithe, 5-foot-11-inch, athletic frame, was accentuated by a full head of jet black hair which in a short time had reached his shoulders. He was a turn-of-the-century "hippie" and the people loved it. Unlike his counterparts of the 60's he wasn't a "greaser." He was an immaculate gentleman. His hair was brushed to a high sheen and his clothes, highlighted by a Prince Albert coat, were always clean and meticulously pressed.

Once his church was completed, to the raves of his congregation and the press, he set out on a campaign of filling its 1,800 seats for every Sunday service. This included bringing exotic animals and birds into the pulpit to attract attention. He succeeded in getting permission from the local zoo for the loan of eagles, bears, deer and anything else which would bring the crowds. He really didn't care why they came to church as long as they did and heard the Gospel. He held the congregation spellbound with his preaching. His oratory was electrifying.

Smith benefited from this association. Right from his first Sunday he began taking his turn in the pulpit. Before many days had passed Morrow had him on the street corners caging donations from the public.

The very first sermon Smith preached at Dale smacked of the sensational. At least the advertisement on the church page hinted at something special.

Toronto Telegram, Saturday, June 5, 1915

CHURCH SERVICES SUNDAY, JUNE 6, 1915

DALE CHURCH

11:00 a.m., Rev. Mr. Morrow
will show a living
eagle to the children

— — —

7:00 p.m., Rev. Oswald J. Smith
will preach on
"THE CHRIST LIFE"

This is Mr. Smith's first
Sunday as Associate Pastor
and every member should
be at this important service.

Smith always considers Dale his first pastorate. The previous pastorates in Chicago, Belwood and Garafraxa, were interim and served two purposes . . . experience and money.

He learned from each appointment but, because he was a student during each pastorate, he didn't involve himself too closely with the administration. He preached and ministered. The business was looked after by the elders or deacons. At Dale it was different. He was both minister and administrator.

Morrow was not one to keep the reins of power to himself as is the case with many ministers who have assistants. The pattern sometimes takes the same form as the American Presidency where the vice-president often complains, following his leaving office, that he was never told anything or brought into the confidence of his chief.

Morrow, to his credit, kept Smith in the picture at all times. This included complete briefings on all church problems. He held nothing back. This total involvement grounded

Smith in the art of handling people. He learned from Morrow that no part is bigger than the whole and regardless of who is involved nothing should come between the church and its ultimate goal of reaching the lost for Christ. On more than one occasion he marveled at how Morrow brought contentious issues to a head and settled them once and for all.

"I had never seen anything like it before in any church," recalls Smith. "Because of Morrow's flair for the unexpected he was bound to attract criticism. On more than one occasion it could have meant the finish of a lesser man. When situations arose, Morrow told me that he always met them head-on and either settled them or laid his job on the line. He might have disenchanted some of his followers, but he never lost their respect. I learned from him the necessity of keeping my eyes on God and doing my best to protect His work at all times. It hasn't been easy, but I've never regretted some of the decisions I've had to make. Many times when I was faced with a problem I'd think back to the days when I was with Morrow and wonder what he'd do. I'd like to think that, if he were in my place, he'd do exactly what I did."

During the period that "Ben" and Alice Smith were starting their family in the small hamlet of Odessa, George and Mary Billings were establishing themselves in Peterborough, 100 miles west.

Peterborough, in the heart of Ontario's Kawartha District, is an ideal spot in which to bring up a family. It is surrounded by beautiful lakes and rolling countryside. The third child of what was a family of six was a petite little girl. Her name was Daisy, nothing more. The simplicity of her name was to become evident years later when she applied for a passport. For years she had called nerself Daisy Mabel Billings but, when the records were searched, she was just plain Daisy Billings. It seems that her uncle who was given the responsibility of registering her birth decided that two Christian names were unnecessary since all you ever used was just one so . . . Daisy Billings it was. She was bright, intelligent and quick.

Some people make a hobby out of connecting unrelated events with improbable happenings and coming up with interesting tales of human involvement. An excellent example of this would be in the early patterns of Daisy Billings and Oswald Smith.

Both were born in Ontario within a hundred miles of each other and grew up in the same social element. The similarity ends there, until years later when the long arm of coincidence reappears.

The Billings family of Peterborough was a fun-loving God-fearing middle class household. The father, a mill worker, left the house early in the morning and returned late at night to provide for his family. The mother worked hard for her children and each one remembers her as a kindly woman, dependable and loving.

The Billings' family were regular members of the Christian and Missionary Alliance Church and it was at the age of nine that Daisy gave her life to Christ. She had heard the way of salvation presented under the ministry of Dr. R. J. Zimmerman, a legend in the C.M.A. denomination.

Following her conversion she became determined to enter into full-time service and all her energies were directed in that area.

Nine years later, when she was eighteen, she entered the Nyack Missionary Institute in upper New York State and began studying for Christian service.

After three years training she graduated and with a friend and fellow student, Ada Loose, began her practical work.

The similarity between the two young lives becomes evident once again. Instead of heading for Toronto or a Canadian mission field, Daisy and Ada emulated Smith by picking the United States. Their destination was a little town called Roaring Fork in the mountains of Virginia. The mountain folk of that state were equally as backward and neglected as the mountaineers of Kentucky.

The girls worked hard to bring a semblance of physical and spiritual comfort to their people wherever possible. Since they had a two-fold ministry, covering both the practical and spiritual, they were called upon to assist in many unusual ways. Once, when a baby died, Daisy was elected to be undertaker and preacher. She dressed the small body, placed it in a rough hewn coffin, and conducted the funeral service. It was their willingness to become involved with the sorrows of the community that endeared the two young Canadian girls to their people.

Their missionary work was cut short by the death of Ada's mother. Upon returning to Canada, Daisy applied for deaconess training and was accepted by a Toronto based Mission Board. Following graduation, she was employed by Reverend J. D. Morrow and became senior deaconess at Dale Presbyterian Church.

For the next two years she served Dale and her Lord with distinction. Morrow was enthusiastic about the work and capabilities of Daisy Billings. "She is the best deaconess in Canada," he once said.

She became a familiar figure in her dainty deaconess uniform, as she moved about the district visiting, counseling and helping wherever and whenever the opportunity presented itself.

One morning Morrow called Daisy into his office and asked her to sit down. This was rather unusual because he was a man of action and usually conducted his conversations on the run.

"Miss Billings," he said, "I feel the time has come in the growth of our church when the work now calls for a full-fledged minister to assist me. This will also help you because it will release you from much of the administrative load you are now carrying. It will permit you to return to your duties as deaconess. I know just the man. His name is Oswald Smith. What do you think?"

Daisy shifted her weight and tugging at the sleeves of her uniform replied, "Oh no, I think it would be very unwise to take anyone on full-time until he had proved himself first. What if he didn't work out?"

Recalling the conversation years later she said, "I was more concerned with my position than whether or not this new fellow would fit in. I'd worked hard to get where I was and I had no intention of letting anyone upset my way of life. In plain words, I resented the fact that Morrow even thought he needed someone else."

Despite her reservations, Morrow brought Smith into Dale

as an equal partner. He was determined that Daisy and Oswald would work harmoniously together and decided to get things off on the right foot. A private dinner in his home would be an ideal way to make introductions, he decided. Wanting Daisy to make a good impression he discreetly suggested that she dress up for the occasion and just this once, forget her uniform.

"The very fact that he asked me to leave it off made me wear it. I wasn't particularly interested in making an impression anyway. I was sure this Smith fellow wasn't going to work out," she said. "I took the street car to Morrow's house and never noticed the tall, gaunt, young man as he got off at the same stop. I started up the street and, as I turned into the walk leading to the Morrow house, I was conscious that someone was beside me."

Smith recalls the occasion well. "I saw her on the street car and decided that she must be Daisy Billings. I doubt if I would have given her a second thought except that she was wearing her uniform. I wondered at a young woman wearing it for a social occasion, but figured that was her business. As we got up to Morrow's house I thought it would be easier if I introduced myself and broke the ice. 'You must be Miss Billings,' I said, 'I'm Oswald Smith.' It wasn't exactly what you'd call a clever opening, but it was a start."

Morrow was not one to waste words, especially when he was setting a situation in its proper perspective. As he opened the door and saw Oswald and Daisy the thought ran through his mind that he really had a unique pair of co-workers: a deaconess just over 5 feet tall who weighed 95 pounds and an assistant who was 6 feet tall and at 120 pounds looked as thin as a bean pole.

"Well, I didn't know you knew each other. I see you are starting out together; let's hope you end together. Just one thing I must ask of you both, at no time must you be seen together by the congregation. All your dealings with each other must be strictly on a business basis."

"You have nothing to worry about," mumbled Daisy under her breath.

The dinner and evening went off exceptionally well. Smith

watched the deaconess at every opportunity and gradually fell under her spell. She was gracious, a good conversationalist, and appeared to be wholly dedicated to her work, Dale Presbyterian and above all, loyal to Morrow who she respected as a man and revered as a minister.

That evening was a high point for Smith. "I remember going home after the dinner and wondering how I could see her socially and yet obey Morrow's instructions. I decided to combine business with pleasure. It took some doing, but I was soon able to dig up enough business that I had to call on her every night. After all, the work had to come first and we were co-workers!"

Besides their "business meetings" at night, Oswald and Daisy saw each other every day. It is only natural that before too long a personal involvement began to develop. They followed Morrow's orders and the only time they were seen together in public was when they rode in a horse and buggy during the funeral processions for the Dale members.

"I always felt sorry for the family when someone passed away," smiled Daisy. "I wasn't too disappointed at being seen in public with Oswald. In fact, I rather enjoyed it. Dale had a lot of funerals during those days . . . we attended every one."

Smith's first year at Dale was a paradox. He was enthused at being a part of such a great work and learned much from his association with Morrow. Because he was an equal partner he was permitted to share the pulpit on alternate services. This was the experience he wanted. When he preached Morrow listened intently. He brought out the best in his young associate as he gently and not so gently rounded off the rough edges with his criticism and suggestions. When Morrow preached, Smith felt he was back in a classroom. He watched and learned how this master communicator reached a congregation and held it. Sometimes he would break into a song right in the middle of a sermon. If that didn't work, he'd lower his voice to a whisper and end up with everyone sitting on the edges of their seats, afraid that they would miss something important.

The elders at Dale were not always behind Morrow, or

for that matter Smith, 100 per cent. There was a hard-core element who viewed their straight-line preaching and evangelism with reserved enthusiasm. Morrow knew what was simmering just below the surface and more than once Smith saw him rise to the occasion and settle a contentious situation. Sometimes it resulted in a showdown and the dissident one either retrenched or resigned his membership. Morrow's life as a minister at Dale was not particularly smooth but he never complained or thought it would be.

By the fall of 1915 Smith's health had become a cause of concern. He tried one doctor after another, plus a succession of home remedies, as he desperately sought relief from constant headaches and unrelieved lethargy. By the spring of 1916 he had reached such a state of physical exhaustion that he found it impossible to continue his duties. It was obvious that Smith needed a complete break from the routine so Morrow suggested he take a leave of absence. Reluctant to do so, but realizing that if he didn't regain his health it could mean the finish of his ministry, Smith agreed, and left for Clifton Springs, New York, and a complete rest.

The fall and winter months had been difficult ones for everyone involved with the work. Besides the responsibilities of ministering to the congregation every spare moment was taken up with the building program.

On April 2, 1916, the completed church was formally opened and received unqualified acceptance from both the congregation and the press.

The Evening Telegram covered the dedication service in depth. Its feature headline was: "DALE'S GREAT DAY DAWNS . . . Roofless No More."

Reporters from the other Toronto papers were equally as flattering. One writer led off his story with: "Opening recognized as a personal achievement of Pastor Rev. J. D. Morrow."

Probably the best report began with: "A great achievement, large congregation gathers for worship in beautiful edifice."

Unfortunately, Smith missed the memorable occasion. He was still recuperating in Clifton Springs. Daisy Billings, however, took a major role in the official program. She preached the final service in the church basement, an honor which was granted her in recognition of the outstanding contributions she had made over the two years she was at Dale.

The weeks of withdrawal from responsibility and complete rest worked wonders. Completely restored to good health, Smith returned to Toronto and Dale ready to resume his work. Morrow was delighted to have him back . . . and so was Daisy.

During the months which had passed since that first meeting they had been drawn together by a bond of mutual love and respect. Daisy was everything that Smith looked for in a woman.

"She was exactly what I wanted for a wife. Every day that I saw her convinced me more and more that God had brought us together for a purpose."

"I wasn't surprised that things were working out this way," recalled Daisy. "When I heard that he was coming and was around my own age I had a feeling that I was going to marry him. Don't ask me how, I just knew. It's one of those things that women sometimes know. You can be sure I never told Oswald until years later. They say it's a wise woman who keeps the men guessing. I've never heard what they say about a man who keeps a woman guessing. Oswald never let on to me that he was serious until one day when he took me to see a house."

Smith remembers the incident and whenever he recalls it has to smile at the way he took Daisy and her feelings for granted.

"I had wanted to get a place of my own for some time. The streetcar ride was too long from where I was living and it wasn't particularly quiet for studying or reading. I'd made up my mind that I wanted to marry Daisy, but somehow neglected to tell her. I just took for granted that she knew what I was thinking. I had a certain style of house in mind and wandered all over Toronto looking for it. When I finally found one that suited me and made the necessary financial arrangements, I asked Daisy to look it over and let me know if she liked it. The woman who owned the house, a Mrs. English, mistook Daisy for my wife and asked her if she was Mrs. Smith. Daisy set her straight in no uncertain terms by saying, 'I'm Miss

Billings, the deaconess. Mr. Smith just asked me to see the house and give my opinion.' She really made no mistake and emphasized who she was by slowly and clearly enuniciating each syllable of the Miss Billings. It was not until much later that she told me she really thought I had another girl in mind and wondered at me asking her in the first place. I can't imagine how she ever thought there was someone else. I suppose I didn't understand women too well at that point. Come to think of it, I don't think I understand them any better now."

The house at 58 Garden Avenue in Toronto's west end was ideal. It was a two-story solid brick house with seven rooms and two open-grate fireplaces . . . a good family house. Smith arranged for terms of $300.00 per year principal and interest and closed the deal at a purchase price of $4,000. The same house today would probably bring close to $20,000 on the inflated real estate market. He was sure that with close budgeting, his $1,000 yearly salary could be stretched to look after the expenses of a wife and home.

Once the details were settled Smith began to court Daisy in earnest. On the evening of June 2nd he took her canoeing on the Humber River and asked her to accept his ring. Elated that she reciprocated his love, he returned to his room and wrote a touching tribute to the woman who was to be his wife for over 50 years.

"Only a Ring" has four verses. The first one conveys the love and devotion he offered her that day and has showered down on her through the years of happily married life.

> 'Twas only a ring that I gave you, dear
>   'Neath the light of the stars above,
> And oh, it seemed such a little thing,
>   But it sealed, it sealed our love;
> Then wear it, dear, while the years go by,
>   My own true love forever;
> And from that hour that made us one
>   May naught arise to sever.

On September 12, 1916, Daisy Billings and Oswald Smith were married in Dale Presbyterian Church. J. D. Morrow conducted the ceremony assisted by John McNichol. *The Telegram* covered the event and ran the following story:

Seldom has Toronto seen a larger wedding than the one last evening when about two thousand people crowded into the new Dale Presbyterian Church to witness the marriage of its beloved deaconess, Miss Daisy Billings, third child of Mr. and Mrs. George Billings, Dufferin Street, to Rev. Oswald J. Smith, the assistant pastor of the church and son of Mr. and Mrs. B. Smith. Rev. J. D. Morrow, assisted by Rev. J. McNichol, performed the ceremony which took place on the pulpit platform. The bride was prettily attired in a cream serge suit with blue silk trimmings and a hat to match, and wore a corsage bouquet of roses. The bride entered the church on the arm of her father to the strains of the wedding march played by Miss Lorna Hughes. During the signing of the registry Mr. McBretney sang "All Joy Be Thine." Messrs. John Porter and Fred Rutherford were ushers. Mr. and Mrs. Smith later left directly for Quebec and other eastern points and on their return will reside at 58 Garden Avenue.

"Plain Daisy Smith mightn't be much of an improvement over plain Daisy Billings," said Mrs. Smith as she neared her fifty-third wedding anniversary, "but I've never been sorry. If I had to do it all over again I'd change nothing. I've enjoyed being plain Daisy Smith."

Smith when he was in charge of Dale Presbyterian
(he was 25 years old at the time)

Chapter 10

Despite the countless thousands who have seen him on the platform and heard him preach there are few who really know Oswald J. Smith. Many of his own congregation, who have followed him from one church to another, still regard him as a distant, coldly detached preacher whom God has used despite himself. They have never seen the other side which is shy, warm, humorous, tender and very easily hurt. That "other" side comes across distinctly in his personal diary which he guards as closely as if it were the crown jewels.

The entries covering his ministry at Dale Presbyterian are a case in point. Many times, he was so completely beside himself in the joy of the Lord, that it was barely possible for him to fully express his feelings. Other times, his despair was so pronounced that it even affected his handwriting.

Any art student will tell you that Vincent Van Gogh, the Dutch painter, was transparent because the strokes of his brush betrayed his emotions. In this regard, Smith is not unlike Van Gogh.

On September 24, 1917 in a scrawling hand he wrote, "Greatly discouraged over last night's service. Things seemed so dead, almost like a stone. I had no liberty, no power, no freedom to preach. Hard, hard, hard, felt like I was just playing with the message."

On October 5th the firm, clear handwriting confirmed his exalted spirits. "Spent yesterday in prayer, on my face before God. How wonderfully He has opened His Word while in prayer."

Again on October 10th he wrote in a well defined hand. "Had a better prayer meeting tonight. The people testified for over half an hour and I had to step in and lead them to prayer. God is really working. Conviction is spreading and lives are being changed. Souls are coming into a glorious relationship with the Saviour. God's Word is becoming so precious."

These entries, while only two weeks apart in time, were miles apart in emotion. Such hills and valleys were bound to have an effect on Smith and his congregation . . . they did.

By September 1916 Europe was in the grip of a bloody war. Great Britain and her Empire were reeling from a series of major setbacks on the battlefields of Europe. The Battle of the Somme, which began on July first, had weakened both the Allies and Germans alike. Since the United States was not to enter the conflict until April the following year, reinforcements had to be drawn from Empire countries, already seriously drained of their youth.

John Morrow was acutely conscious of the grim situation and, as soon as his church was completed, joined up.

The Telegram paid him the singular honor of running a feature story about his enlistment.

Toronto Telegram, September 18, 1916

. REV. J. D. MORROW IN KHAKI

Rev. J. D. Morrow, the 'Athletes' Parson,' has decided to don khaki. From now on he will be known as Capt. J. D. Morrow, and will act as chaplain to the 180th (Sportsmen's) Battalion. This unit is due to leave for Camp Borden in the next few days.

It was not an easy decision for Morrow to make. He had just come through the most hectic years of his ministry. He could not be faulted for thinking that he had every right to enjoy his church and spend a well earned period of just being pastor of the second largest Presbyterian church in Canada. This was not the way Morrow operated. When he realized that there was a need, he met that need head on.

Smith, unable to pass an induction medical because of his health, was the logical man to fill Morrow's place in the pulpit. On October 16th the Session formally placed him in charge of

Dale during Morrow's absence overseas. Smith was just 26 years of age when the appointment was confirmed.

Following his enlistment, Captain Morrow was given a brief embarkation leave before shipping out for England.

"It was an emotion-filled night as he preached his farewell message," recalled Smith. "As soon as he was issued a uniform he had to submit to a military haircut. It was as short as it had been long. Because it had been years since the people had seen him with short hair he was quite nervous and unsure as to how they would accept him. As we waited to go onto the platform he kept running his hand over the short stubble of what was once shoulder-length hair. I thought he looked quite dashing in his uniform and told him so. He seemed reluctant to walk through the curtain which led to the platform. Finally, he told me to go first and, as he followed me out, the great congregation, which packed the auditorium, stood to their feet and burst into applause. It was a thrilling moment. I was proud of Morrow and proud of my country. I'm sure everyone there felt the same way. Following his farewell message, at least seven hundred people who had been in the auditorium walked or drove to Morrow's house on Roxton Road and sang 'God be With You Till We Meet Again.' The tribute was so remarkable that the papers carried the complete story of the service and the emotional display of his congregation which stopped traffic on the street in front of his house."

Morrow was so overcome that words failed him and all he could do was hold his wife's hand and nod thanks to those who came.

"If anything happens to me," he said, his eyes brimming with tears, "I ask you to keep Dale Church a people's church. I always want it to be a place where people can go to hear the real Gospel, where the 'down-and-outs' may feel there is a welcome for them."

It was to be two years before Morrow addressed his congregation again.

The next two years at Dale were really the making of Smith. The church was, in effect, a split congregation. It was not split in the usual sense, rather split on definition, as to exactly what was wanted or expected from the minister. One segment wanted what Smith and his predecessor were offering . . . sound evangelical preaching based on a Bible-believing concept which included salvation and a separated life. For the other schismatic body, this was completely unacceptable. They based their objection on the fact that Smith's ministry contradicted, and took exception to, their liberal attitudes. Most of the men were lodge members and lived a more wide-open type of life than Smith was preaching. They had no compunction about smoking, dancing, attending the theatre or social drinking. Smith would not, or could not, moderate his ministry so that it would be in harmony with this attitude. As was to be expected, unrest and dissension broke out.

The more Smith felt he was being attacked the more his group rallied around, vindicating his stand.

"It was a time of great testing, but as always God worked wonders. Perhaps if I had not been put through those trials I might never have been driven to the point of being burdened for souls and revival at Dale. Day after day I met with my band of faithful members and we prayed for God's blessing."

It really began on August 16, 1917, when Smith wrote in his diary, "It must come, the revival for which I've prayed."

The break came on September 11th. "Glory be to God!" he recorded. "There has been a move at last. It occurred in the cottage prayer meeting tonight."

For the next 12 months, his diary is filled with one story after another of those who found their way to Christ. Many were "one time wonders" but there were also many who were genuinely saved and remained true to their faith for the years to come. It shook up Dale to such an extent that those who believed in revival, and what Smith stood for, had their faith restored or strengthened. Those who didn't, form another story.

Out of the "Awakening at Dale," as Smith calls those months, came one of his most widely used hymns, "A Revival Hymn." The title is self-explanatory and the message, plain and moving. This is perhaps the reason why it has remained so popular down through the years. It leaves absolutely no question in the mind of the singer or listener. The message applied to Dale in 1916 and certainly applies to The Peoples Church in 1969 — and any other church for all the years to come. A full account of the Dale Revival is in the last three chapters of Smith's book, *Passion for Souls*.

> Revive Thy work, O Lord!
>> And manifest Thy pow'r;
> Oh come upon Thy church and give
>> A penitential show'r!

> Revive Thy work, O Lord,
>> Come now and answer prayer;
> O come in Holy Spirit pow'r,
>> And save men ev'rywhere.

On March 31, 1918, at the end of the revival, Morrow returned to his wife Edith and their three children, Hugh, Ives and Genevieve. Mrs. Morrow and Ives are deceased. The remaining two children reside with their families in Toronto. Morrow was an emotionally and physically spent man as nearly 3,000 people packed Dale's auditorium to welcome him home. The papers covered the service and the Telegram ran the following account:

Toronto Telegram, Monday, April 1, 1918

MANY IN AUDIENCE WEPT

VIVID PICTURE OF SCENE AT THE FRONT, TOLD BY
CAPT. MORROW, IS TOO MUCH FOR GIRL.

With tense, tear-stained faces the big congregation in Dale Church last night heard (Capt.) Rev. J. D. Morrow the pastor, just returned from England and France, tell the story of the death of a young Canadian soldier, Private Evans.

The service was in the hands of Rev. Oswald Smith, the associate pastor. It was the largest crowd in the history of the church . . .

Morrow's return was short-lived. He never really took up the reins of the pastorate again. It was not long until he left Toronto for California, never to return. His health had been broken due to the trials of serving overseas and on April 28, 1921, he passed away at the age of 48. Smith is convinced that, had he lived and continued on in the ministry, he might have become one of Canada's greatest evangelists.

The next six months, from April to October, were difficult ones for Smith, more difficult than he had ever believed possible. He had just seen the church revitalized through revival and honestly thought that those who were hardened against his particular style of preaching might soften. Instead, the situation deteriorated until the climax came on October 15th when Smith tendered his resignation to the Session . . . it was accepted.

The unrest which had been fermenting before and after Morrow's return, found its roots in the dissentient faction of the church. They made a presentation to the Session and when all the frills and platitudes were stripped away it boiled down to their displeasure at:

1) The revival meetings which Smith conducted. They found them an irritation.
2) The selection of gospel hymns which were being used. They preferred the staid, old-time selections.
3) The prayer meetings — they didn't think they were necessary or particularly useful.
4) The $600.00 Smith raised for missions. They strongly objected to his continual emphasis on foreign missions.

It was the last charge which Smith now considers the most ludicrous.

"The very thing in which I've immersed nearly 60 years of service was the thing that sealed my doom at Dale. They used to call me and my faithful followers, 'Mr. Smith and his soul-saving gang.' This really upset some of the older Saints in the group and one time, after a particularly vicious attack, I calmed them by telling them we were fortunate. Surely the servants of God could hardly covet more. We were highly honored, I said."

Smith faithfully carried out his pastoral duties in the face of all this opposition. Morrow was in evidence, but his health prohibited him from entering actively into the controversy. It was as distressing for him as it was for Smith.

From April 1st to his final service on October 27th, Smith preached 49 sermons in the main auditorium. He knew that his tenure was short and unlike many who would have written off the entire situation he kept hammering away right up to the end. His very sermon titles highlighted the despair in his heart as he saw the congregation that he loved so desperately, spiritually slipping away before his very eyes:

"The Need of Salvation"
"Deliverance"
"The Need of More Prayer"
"Saving Faith"
"Holiness Of Life"
"My Master"
"God So Loved That He Gave"

His final sermon was the clincher that summed up his entire ministry at Dale: "You Need Jesus."

Smith's entry in his diary on October 27th was brief and to the point. "My last service is ended and I'm out of Dale at last. We had an enormous audience, taking everything into consideration."

His first professional pastorate ended.

It was just nine days following his final sermon at Dale that one of those strange quirks of fate took place. On November 5th, the Presbytery of Toronto officially received him into their communion, granting him full recognition as a minister of the Presbyterian Church of Canada. He has never resigned from the denomination although for the most part his ministry has been completely outside the Presbyterian church.

Had he been single, Smith would not have been so concerned for the future. He was now, however, a husband and father with a year-old son, Glen Gilmour. Glen was born on June 22, 1917, and Smith felt his parental responsibilities keenly. With no money saved he could not afford to be without a paying job. Knowing that his days at Dale were numbered he put out feelers and was approached by the pulpit committee of Beulah Tabernacle in Toronto. Beulah was a small gospel church which had its beginning with the Plymouth Brethren. He was sure that these godly people wouldn't present any spiritual or scriptural road-blocks to his ministry so he decided to accept their invitation for the month of November at least. His ministry at Beulah lasted from November, 1918, to the end of February, 1919. It was a brief but fruitful ministry. The only disappointment was in the denominationalism which some of its members exhibited. Coupled with his experiences at Dale and a church hierarchy, Smith's exposure to this type of organization started him thinking. He wondered if it would be possible to form a work which would be completely scriptural in concept and not be hampered by some absolute authority. He wanted freedom from an elected body which could hamstring him with old, time-honored but archaic denominational precepts. It was just an idea, but it had planted itself in his subconscious and would come to the surface at a later date.

During the four months at Beulah he had the opportunity to attend a series of meetings called "A Victorious Life Conference." The main speaker was Dr. Charles G. Trumbull, then the editor of *The Sunday School Times*. He also attended meetings held by the American evangelist Paul Rader who was later to become his confidant and friend. These meetings filled a deep need in his life. After Dale he had virtually lived in a spiritual vacuum. These two men brought a renewed vitality to his personal life and ministry.

It was at the Paul Rader meetings that Smith was approached by William Henderson, the Founder and Superintendent of the Shantymen's Christian Association. He told Smith about the plans the Shantymen had to open up their ministry in British Columbia. The Shantymen's Association, which still has an active ministry to the loggers and lumberjacks of Canada's vast forest regions, had heard about Smith's experiences and success as a colporteur for the Bible Society on the Canadian west coast. Henderson was very persuasive and shot down any arguments Smith raised. He reasoned that everything has a purpose, and it was obviously God's purpose that he finish his ministry in Toronto exactly at the time someone with his experience was needed by the Shantymen. Smith had no defense. On March 21st he, along with Daisy and the year-and-a-half-old Glen, boarded the train at Toronto's Union Station and headed for the West. It was just eleven years since he had left B.C. for the east and now he was returning as a seasoned minister, evangelist and Bible scholar.

Chapter 11

Leaving Toronto wasn't an easy decision for Smith to make. He was established with his wife and child in the first home they had ever owned. Now he would have to sell it. Unlike some itinerant ministers and evangelists who pack up and go at a moment's notice, Smith weighed the alternatives carefully. He had no intention of jeopardizing his son's future by dragging him all around the country while he preached at one church after another. Convinced that he was being led of God he placed his house up for sale and made the necessary arrangements to leave Toronto for British Columbia. Fortunately, a buyer appeared for his house and even more fortunately, he was able to sell it for $4,300.00 — a modest appreciation of $300.00.

"In reading countless biographies of great men who have been used of God down through the years I've been struck by the fact that many have made very poor husbands and fathers," says Smith. "It is not uncommon to read of men who pioneered great revivals and at the same time lost all contact with their children. Many have publicly regretted keeping their wives and children with them as they traveled. They realized, too late, that it is far better to establish a home and give the family roots. I had no intention of letting it happen to me. I only decided to take Daisy and Glen with me on this occasion because he was just a little over a year old. I intended to get them settled in Vancouver before I ever started my work for the Shantymen."

Following their arrival in Vancouver on April 1, 1919,

Smith registered in the Alczar Hotel. After a couple of days he found a small, two-room, basement apartment . . . much to the relief of his wife. Mothers, with babies in diapers, can appreciate her peace of mind at getting into any living quarters, even if it was just a basement apartment. It didn't take long to find out that basement apartments and Vancouver's climate are not compatible. Because of the excessive dampness, Smith had to look for more comfortable accommodation. Fortunately it didn't take too long before he located exactly what they wanted. Better still, it was at a figure which didn't place too much strain on their limited budget. For $50.00 a month he was able to rent a completely furnished house.

Once Daisy and Glen were settled he turned his full attention to the Shantymen and his duties of preaching the Gospel to a needy and forgotten section of Canada's society.

He was with the Shantymen for five months, much shorter than the last time he had ministered on the west coast. There were a number of similarities this time but also a number of differences. He retraced many familiar miles once again as he visited some of the lumber camps and communities he remembered so well. Names such as Hartley Bay, Prince Rupert and Fort Simpson reappear in his diary as he wrote about the excitement of seeing old acquaintances and renewing friendships. The difference this time was in having sympathetic company.

"Altogether, I made seven missionary journeys up the British Columbia coast. I was very grateful to God that He permitted me to be associated with four of the most dedicated workers it's been my privilege to know: William Henderson, Alex Weir, Jim Matheson and Dr. E. Ralph Hooper. Dr. Hooper was a Toronto physician who heeded God's call to the mission field and gave up a lucrative practice to work with the lumberjacks and loggers. We had to travel by steamer, logging train, canoe and sometimes, we even walked the log booms. It was much easier this time because I had company. If anyone doubts the value of such companionship they don't realize what those camps were like. The men were rough, hard and indifferent. They lived a lonely, secluded womenless life with nothing much to do in their spare time except gamble, drink and brawl. Anyone new in camp was immediately considered to be fair game. There was hardly a camp visited that didn't have a local joker whose main enjoyment was making us the point of his jest. Despite the insults and rebuffs we were able to see some returns for our efforts. Any positive decisions, or even sparks of interest, were cherished because nothing came easy. I'm sure that if I had been alone I wouldn't have lasted."

Smith had many thrilling experiences and was often to thank God for His providential care. On one particular evening in July after Smith and his companion, Dr. Hooper, had hiked twelve miles through the bush, they found every bunk filled at the camp. It was well after midnight and they were bone-tired. After wandering around the camp wondering what to do or where to sleep, they found a pile of old mattresses. Digging out four of the best ones they carried them down to the beach of the Pacific Ocean and fashioned a makeshift bed, using one of the mattresses as a cover.

"It was one of most delightful sleeps I've ever had," recalled Smith.

It is an accepted fact that the human body is conditioned to reject pain and retain pleasant experiences. Fortunately for Smith this is the case because, instead of remembering his days with the Shantymen as ones of personal abuse by a group of uncouth and blasphemous men, he looks back on them as spiritually rewarding. In fact, he has never forgotten the afternoon of July 11th:

"Dr. Hooper and I had arrived at a place called Jackson Bay where we planned to hold some meetings. It had been our practice to get away by ourselves for prayer before each service. This time we had made our way up the trail about a mile from the logging camp. We found that the only way we could face the men was to pray for special strength. It was all that kept us going. A large tree had fallen across the gully so we walked out on the trunk and knelt to pray. It was an ideal setting in which to reach out to God. The primeval forest, rimmed by the mountain peaks, framed the two of us as we turned our faces up to Heaven.

"God came very near to both of us that day. I was com-

119

pletely taken over by His presence and clearly saw a vision of Toronto. I know that visions are not popular with certain segments of the Christian church, but nevertheless, I had a vision that day. I saw the multitude of lost souls and felt a direct call to return and open up an independent work which would reach them all. It was an unmistakable call and I've never doubted for a moment that God was speaking directly to me."

That experience was followed by another just four weeks later on August 27th.

The entry in his diary fairly bristles with excitement: "I prayed the prayer of Paul today, 'Lord, what wilt Thou have me to do?' I got my answer clear and unmistakable. 'Arise and go into the city and it shall be told thee what thou must do.' I immediately visualized myself in Toronto calling the people back to God . . . I have to return."

He finished his term with the Shantymen and made his way as quickly as possible to Vancouver. Without further delay the necessary arrangements were completed for the return to Toronto and what he fully expected would be his life's work.

The dictionary defines faith as: "a complete confidence in someone or something." That definition describes exactly Smith's state of mind as he and his wife and child stepped off the train in Toronto's Union Station. He didn't have any idea of what he would be doing or, more important, of how he would even support his family. Nevertheless, he was full of expectation, believing that he was in God's will and everything would be opened up to him.

"I didn't have any idea of exactly what I was supposed to do. After Daisy and Glen were settled I contacted the Shantymen and they sent me to Northern Ontario and a few week's work among the lumber camps. It wasn't exactly what I had come east for, but it filled the gap until I had a more direct leading . . . it also paid."

Once the weather closed in, he returned to Toronto for what he hoped would be a short wait. The waiting stretched into days, then into weeks and finally into months without anything definite. Never being a man noted for patience he found the inactivity and uncertainty almost unbearable. He would pace back and forth in constant prayer, desperately trying, as it were, to force God's hand. He was later to look back on those months as a great experience. At the time they were completely intolerable.

Financially he was in pretty good circumstances. Following his return from Northern Ontario he was appointed to the part-time editorial staff of the *Evangelical Christian*, a monthly magazine, at $15.00 a week. He was also made Secretary of the Shantymen's Christian Association at $20.00 a week. This brought his weekly income up to a respectable $35.00. He was able to live quite comfortably on that amount, but was soon to need every additional cent. On February 4, 1920, his only daughter, Hope Evangeline, was born.

"Daisy and I picked Evangeline for a second name because Longfellow's Evangeline was our favorite poem and many times we would read it out loud to each other."

Smith's taste in literature runs from poetry to prose. He lists his favorite poets in this order:

POET	POEM
Alfred Lord Tennyson	*In Memoriam*
Henry Wadsworth Longfellow	*Evangeline*
John Greenleaf Whittier	*Our Master*

When asked to name his favorite author and piece of literature Smith, without hesitation, lists James Fenimore Cooper and *The Last of the Mohicans* first, closely followed by Alexander Dumas and his classic, *The Count of Monte Cristo*.

"I've read these books over and over again and never cease to marvel at the skill of these writers as they wove their characters in and out of powerful conflicts.

"These men also wrote strong religious convictions into their books. I feel sorry for those who have never taken the time or interest to read literature of this type. They don't know what they are missing."

To fill in time and augment his income, Smith preached wherever and whenever the invitation was offered. His sermon diary lists the wide range of pulpits occupied during those days: Wychwood Disciples; Beulah Tabernacle; Olivet Baptist; Central Methodist; Knox Presbyterian; Caroline Street Mission and Evangel Hall. Instead of weakening his ministry the reverse was the case. He had to be in "top form" at all services and, as a result, probably unconsciously, prepared more diligently, preached more forcefully and put out the extra effort that a minister, who is secured in a pastorate, sometimes can overlook. His sermons, while certainly not cerebral, had a quality about them which attracted the average church-goer. Smith never particularly cared for, or even attempted, to present a definitively intellectual message. Instead, his forte has been in the simplicity of the Gospel. This worked for him in British Columbia, it was the right approach in Kentucky, and he was satisfied that it was meeting the challenge of the times. It was the only way he knew how to preach. His sermon titles were equally brief and to the point. Instead of using cliches, he relied on self-explanatory topics such as: Wholly God's, God's Purpose for This Age, Prayer, The Way of Life, and Good News. He was to save the gimmicks for later when he had to fill auditoriums night after night during crusades or missionary conventions.

The year 1920 was a hard one for Armenia. The country was gripped in one of the most vicious and devastating famines of its history. Coupled with constant political unrest, and attacks from Turkey, its people were being decimated, seemingly without anyone in the more prosperous countries even caring, much less lifting a finger to help. *The Globe,* Toronto's influential morning paper, decided that the Armenian crisis would be a worthwhile cause to champion. It had rich human interest possibilities and would sell papers which, after all, was what *The Globe* was in business to do.

The editor, Stewart Lyons, decided to approach the subject from a different angle by not assigning a staff writer. A few weeks before, Smith had written and sold a feature to *The Globe* for $10.00 and Lyons was sufficiently impressed to ask him to submit more. The article was entitled "The High Rigger" and centered around some of Smith's experiences and impressions while he was on the west coast. Recalling this article, the editor once again contacted Smith and asked him if he would like to write a series on the Armenian problem. Smith's copy began appearing in the March 1st issue. In vivid prose he outlined the plight of the Armenians and appealed to the general public for donations. Up to that time, he knew little or nothing about Europe or Asia, much less Armenia. In fact, he had to ask where it was and look it up in a world atlas to be sure that such a place really existed. Backed up by the wire stories for research and a helpful editor, his copy caught on and the money flowed in. By the time the public appeal had run its course well over a quarter-of-a-million dollars had been raised which was quickly converted into food, medicine and clothing for Armenian relief. It was a gratifying experience for Smith to see his copy appearing in *The Globe*. It was even more gratifying when he received a total of $50.00 for his efforts. It was a respectable return in a day when experienced writers were making less than that every two weeks.

By the end of May the indecision was driving him to the brink of despair. It wasn't easy on Daisy either, who had her hands full with two small children. He was open to any suggestion and quickly accepted Dr. Hooper's offer to accompany him to Kentucky under sponsorship of the Shantymen's Association and open up a new work with the mountaineers. After saying good-by to Daisy, Glen and Hope, he was once again in Cawood. Unfortunately, Hooper took ill after just a month of hard work and had to return to Toronto. Smith, not wanting to be left alone, came with him. Brief though the ministry had been, the results were significant. During their stay they held 64 services, visited 500 homes and saw 42 decisions for Christ.

Determined to get his ministry in high gear once more, Smith took another giant step in faith. His meager resources prohibited any significant contribution on his behalf no matter how sold he might be on the scheme. If it cost money the finances would have to come from somewhere other than the Smith coffers.

"It was August 26th and a Thursday morning," recalls Smith. "It's funny how certain days stick in your mind. I know it was a Thursday. I was praying and, for the first time in a long while, a new peace and confidence came over me. I felt certain that God's time had come. It had been nearly a year-and-a-half since I had the vision in British Columbia and frankly, I was beginning to have my doubts. On this particular morning all doubts vanished. I knew I was ready to move. I decided that I would launch my second ministry on the first Sunday of October. I had also decided, long ago, to call it 'The Gospel Auditorium.' I picked this name because I wanted everyone who came to know exactly what kind of ministry I was offering. The Gospel would be preached . . . straight and simple."

To compound matters, Smith had accepted two previous bookings to speak elsewhere on the first Sunday of October. He didn't tell anyone about his plans, rather prayed that if God wanted him to go on he would be freed of the obligations. In a few days the booking churches cancelled the engagements of their own accord.

Finances were the next problem. Again Smith told no one, rather committed everything to prayer, an attitude he was to accept with intensity for some time to come.

For the next few weeks it was just a constant revelation of God's hand over the entire endeavor. Dr. Hooper had recovered from his ill health and joined his friend in support. Smith didn't give Hooper any indication as to what he had secretly planned to do. Their fellowship and times of prayer were limited to the seeking of God's blessing on their lives per se. Little did Hooper know at the time the significant role his support and friendship played in Smith's overall plans.

"It didn't take me too long to realize that God was setting His seal of approval on what I was trying to do. I was fortunate in having a friend such as Dr. Hooper. He helped keep me going although I'm sure he didn't realize it. I had begun to pray definitely that the necessary money would come in and waited upon the Lord. It would have been so easy to have gone to a number of my friends and told them what I was trying to do and ask for help. Believe me, I thought of it at times. If I ever had, I would always wonder what God might have done. I'm glad I waited.

"Dr. Hooper was a bit late for our prayer session one day. As soon as he walked into the room I knew something had happened. He had the strangest look on his face as he said, 'Here's something Mr. W. Sneath asked me to give you.' He handed me an envelope and inside was a $10.00 bill. That was the beginning.

"A few days later I was asked to conduct a wedding, the first one I had handled in over a year. I was given $5.00. Finally just a day or so before the first Sunday of October, and the deadline for the beginning of the work, I received a letter with a check for $15.00. A short note accompanied the check which was from a Mr. W. H. Adamson. He wrote, 'I awoke some time during the night and a message, no doubt from God, came to me: send Oswald Smith some money.'

"The day of miracles, at least for me, had not passed. I know that you can pick up any book about the beginning of a church or movement and read accounts of how unexplained and mysterious things happened but you never really come to grips with such experiences until you have become a part of them. For me, the fact that I received a total of $60.00, all completely unsolicited, gave me one of the most thrilling experiences of my Christian life. The amount was exactly what I figured I needed for two weeks expenses. I had found an auditorium I could have for $25.00 a week. It was the old West End Y.M.C.A. with a seating capacity of 750. I wanted at least two weeks finances in advance so that I wouldn't end up being a 'one night wonder.' I finally told Dr. Hooper what had happened over the past few weeks and how he had been a part of God's graciousness. He wasn't as surprised as I thought he might have been. He said God had been speaking to him and he knew there was something going on. He didn't ask questions, just kept the faith. He was the kind of Christian who makes the word meaningful. Many times I've thanked God for men such as Dr. Hooper who have stood with me in prayer when I needed them most."

Hooper was delighted the way things had worked out and offered his full support. Smith designed hand bills, or dodgers as they were sometimes called, and with his companion distributed them door-to-door in the Parkdale area.

Determined to make his church meaningful, Smith formulated a firm constitution which set forth his theology, government and administrative precepts:

ORIGIN . . . Born of God on the 1st Sunday of October, 1920, after almost fifteen months of continuous waiting upon Him in definite, believing prayer, in response to an unmistakable call.

PURPOSE . . . First, a testimony to the faithfulness of God and the reliability of His promises, that He may be glorified. Second, the salvation of souls, the edification of believers and world-wide evangelism.

METHODS . . . First, a work of faith, wholly dependent upon God. Its needs are brought to Him in prayer, and to Him alone. Second, no collections are taken up and no solicitations for funds authorized. Third, no debts are incurred, the work being enlarged only as the Lord indicates His will by sending in the means. Fourth, one-tenth of the total income to be set aside for missions.

The Gospel Auditorium opened its doors on schedule. It is interesting to note that in the constitution two significant conditions are evident . . . one in context and one by omission. Right from the very start of the work Smith set forth his missionary concept so that there would not, or more importantly could not, be any misconception on the part of the adherents as to what role the church would play in this area. The other condition which is unmistakably obvious by its omission is the provision for Smith's salary. It is not mentioned, simply because it was the farthest thing from Smith's mind.

"I was very conscious of the necessity of at least making enough to live on adequately. I've never, in all my life, dictated how much I wanted. Thankfully I've never had to because God has supplied all my needs, more than I could ever ask for, in fact. I felt quite strongly that if He was leading, as He obviously was, everything would be looked after. I didn't have to remind God that I had a wife and two children to provide for. Since the way had been miraculously opened for the start of my church I wasn't going to complicate things by insisting on a salary. I had started in faith and I wasn't going to stop."

Opening night, regardless of what the event, is always a soul-destroying experience for the principals involved.

The service was scheduled to start at 7:00 p.m. and Smith

arrived an hour earlier. As he approached the front entrance and looked up at the large triangular sign which spelled out Y.M.C.A. he was conscious of a cold wave of panic creeping over him. No one was going in!

What if they don't come? he thought.

He looked at the auditorium with its 750 vacant seats and wanted to turn around and run as fast as he could. It was his worst moment. Controlling his emotions, he found a dark corner in an adjoining room and knelt by a chair in prayer. It seemed like an eternity before any sound broke the stillness. He opened his eyes and listened. It sounded like the shuffling of feet. Quietly he eased to the door, opened it, and looked through the crack, afraid of what he was going to see.

"Two men came in and stared at the lower auditorium. I thought they were going to turn around and leave. I really wouldn't have blamed them. Instead of leaving they headed for the stairs and the front of the gallery. I've never been able to figure out why they didn't sit down below. I'd like to think that they decided to get a good seat in case the place would be packed."

By 7:00 o'clock sixty-five had gathered and Smith stood before them to preach the first sermon in The Gospel Auditorium. His sermon topic was "Discipleship" and his text was taken from Luke 14.

It was probably a combination of God's blessing, Smith's preaching and the novelty of something new in the community, that contributed to the success of the fledgling work. Within a few weeks sympathetic Christians offered their services and became active participants. There wasn't any formal membership because Smith didn't want to exclude anyone who had an earnest desire to worship at his church.

"I've always felt that regardless of how loose the conditions of membership may be, someone will feel that they can't comply. I'm not knocking denominations or individual churches which have hard and fast conditions for membership. There is a place for that approach, and many people want it. I was well experienced with the democratic form of church government and saw its weaknesses and strengths. Personally, it was not for me and that is the reason why I've stayed clear of it all these years. I can not find any Scriptural authority which says that you have to have that form of government within the church. Frankly, I'm convinced that the reverse is the case. Someone has to have the final word and even in a democratic church, someone has. I wanted The Gospel Auditorium to be centered on God and not on man, and after all, since I was founding it I figured that this was my prerogative. I prayed about it until I was positive this was God's plan for the work."

Determined to channel everything into the work of the church and not take anything out for himself, Smith made a firm rule. Unless an offering was specifically designated "For Your Personal Use" he wouldn't touch a cent. Little by little the funds came in as the congregation slowly consolidated and grew. Each week the $25.00 rental fee was secured, sometimes just by cents. On the fourth Sunday he was short by $4.82. On the Monday morning he received a $5.00 bill from an anonymous benefactor. That week he had 18¢ left over. Another time, his fortunes improved when he was short exactly $11.02. The offering came to $11.66 which left him 64¢ to spare.

Things were getting desperate in the Smith household. Finances, which had been stretched to the utmost, were finally being strained out of existence. Smith was starting to become unnerved by the constant worry, but he decided to trust God completely and Him alone. One morning in private prayer he made all his needs known. Prayer has sometimes been described as cathartic because the one praying generally feels relieved to get his problems aired if only in private. For Smith it was cathartic in its truest meaning. His fears were calmed and he had that warming peace which a child of God often experiences following introspective prayer.

"I told Daisy that everything was going to be all right . . . and it was."

By the end of October $31.25 came in, marked clearly "For Your Personal Use." November was an improvement as the total rose to $68.33. By the end of December Smith recorded that God had graciously supplied $112.50 for the personal needs of his family.

The Gospel Auditorium had a brief life, just three months. Mid-way in December Smith was in touch with Reverend

A. W. Roffe, the Canadian Superintendent of the Christian and Missionary Alliance. Between the two of them, an amalgamation of The Gospel Auditorium and the Parkdale Tabernacle was hammered out.

On the first Sunday of January, 1921, Smith was installed as the pastor of the Parkdale Tabernacle.

"It made sense to take this step because both churches were in the same area and preached the same Gospel. No matter how long we stayed at The Gospel Auditorium it would still be the Y.M.C.A. in peoples' mind. The Parkdale work was just hanging on by its finger tips. In fact, its congregation was resigned to closing up completely. It was a great opportunity. I knew that my people would come with me and together with the faithful nucleus of Parkdale we could build a work which would glorify God in Toronto's west end."

Smith and first child, Glen, 1917

Daisy Billings at the time of her marriage to Oswald Smith

Chapter 12

The Parkdale Tabernacle was quite a comedown from Dale Presbyterian Church. It was even a comedown from the three-month-old Gospel Auditorium, which is saying something. When Smith mounted the platform for his first sermon he was looking into the faces of only 24 people in the congregation.

With nowhere to go but up, he began his first real attempts at attracting crowds. If he had been in show business his tactics would have branded him as an entrepreneur of the highest rank. He had a gift for drawing people. If he couldn't do it himself he used others.

"I once heard my son Paul say that 'the church is in the business of people and if it doesn't have people it's out of business.' He couldn't have stated it better. I realized that if something wasn't done and do ie quickly Parkdale Tabernacle would soon be dead and I along with it. I committed the matter to prayer and began looking about to see what the possibilities were of coming up with an idea or a workable program. My answer came from two directions . . . the Board of the Christian and Missionary Alliance denomination and Dallas, Texas."

F. F. Bosworth, and his younger brother B. B., had gained a reputation in the early '20's as being two of America's leading evangelists. F. F. was the preacher and B. B. the song leader. They had a unique ability for drawing crowds over a sustained period of time.

130

Realizing that their denomination and many churches in particular, were in dire need of revitalizing, the C. & M. A. Board decided to invite the Bosworths to Toronto for a city-wide evangelistic crusade. It was agreed that the week-night meetings would be held in a local church and the meetings on the weekend would be moved to Massey Hall, which was the only auditorium capable of holding the expected crowds.

Smith was advised that his church, The Parkdale Tabernacle, was chosen for the week-night services and he was directed to act as host minister.

"It was really my first experience with large campaigns," Smith recalls. "F.F. Bosworth was not what you would call a great preacher but he had something. Night after night he would address the people in his quiet manner. His message was Salvation and the Deeper Life. The results were above average as the people responded to the invitation. I was more interested in the mechanics of the crusade than in the actual preaching. I watched and listened carefully. I can honestly thank them for teaching me how to hold extended evangelistic campaigns. I've used some of their techniques down through the years."

On June 1, 1921, the Smith family was completed with the birth of their youngest son and final child, Paul Brainerd. As with Hope, they picked the second name for their son from outside the family. In Paul's case, it was out of respect and admiration for David Brainerd, "The Man of Prayer." In later years Paul was to continue the Smith name in Canadian religious circles. Instead of just being content to follow comfortably in his father's footsteps, he has carved out for himself a reputation as being one of Canada's outstanding evangelical ministers and evangelists.

"It's always difficult not to keep looking upon the last child, especially if he is a boy, as being the baby of the family," says his mother. "Paul was an individualist from the moment he was born. Both Oswald and I knew that he would probably be in the ministry. Unlike Glen, he was outgoing and full of life. Glen was quiet and introverted, usually just content to stay by himself. On the other hand, Paul was always into something. When he was growing up it was just one thing after another. Nothing really bad — he was just all boy. I know it used to bother him when people called him kid brother or baby of the family."

His father began featuring Paul at some of his services from the age of five until he was eleven or twelve. "Once it was obvious that Paul had a better than average voice, I made use of him in as many meetings as I could. The people seemed to enjoy seeing him on the platform. The Los Angeles paper called him 'The Golden Voiced Soloist' after he sang in Trinity auditorium. It was a pretty fair comment on his singing. He appeared in Toronto, Los Angeles, and many other churches around the country."

The success of the Bosworth Brothers just whetted Smith's appetite for large crowds. He had tasted the thrill of being on a platform and in charge of services which attracted capacity audiences. When he saw the crowds being turned away at the doors he knew that this was the ministry he wanted and had no intention of ever being satisfied with anything less. He quickly rationalized that the more people you preach to the more you reach for Christ, and this is to be expected because of his calling. Subconsciously, however, he is not unlike any public figure whether it be theatrical, political or religious, who excels with crowds and dies with empty seats.

Determined not only to maintain his reputation as a crowd-getter but improve upon it, he embarked on yet another scheme to bring people under the sound of the Gospel.

He capitalized on the revival which had begun under the ministry of the Bosworth Brothers eleven weeks earlier. Because of the crowds and excessive summer heat he moved the Parkdale congregation into a large 90' foot square tent which was erected on a vacant lot in mid-town Toronto. The location was significantly better than the Parkdale district because it could be reached equally well from all areas of the city.

Under the auspices of the Christian and Missionary Alliance, and the direction of Smith, the crowds kept coming. Smith was quickly gaining the reputation of being Toronto's most exciting Protestant minister.

"I had heard somewhere that the best way to interest people and create excitement is to get them involved. With this in mind I came up with the idea of having a 'Bring Your Own Chair' shower. I hoped it would provide the tent with seats, save money in the process, and catch the imagination of the people. I promoted this all over the city and it soon caught on. Most of the people who came to the tent services rode on the streetcars and created utter confusion as they tried to maneuver their chairs through a packed tram. There must have been many barked shins and grumbles, but I didn't care. By Sunday morning on July 3, 1921, the tent was completely filled with every kind of kitchen chair imaginable. It had served its purpose.

"I had invited Paul Rader, who by now had become a close friend, to come up from the States and dedicate the tent. I knew that his fiery oratory would keep the revival boiling and that's what I wanted. I was determined to consolidate the gains made over the last eleven weeks and move ahead."

The Telegram ran a feature story about the tent which had become the focal point of evangelism in the city:

DRIVEN BY HEAT TO COOLER TENT
Christian and Missionary Alliance Services Being Held
Under Big Canvas

"The revival which started eleven weeks ago in the Christian and Missionary Alliance Tabernacle, under the preaching of the Bosworth Brothers, was last evening continued in a tent on a vacant lot one block west of Spadina Avenue on College Street.

"Owing to the excessive heat, the meetings in the tabernacle became uncomfortable, and within the past two weeks the people voluntarily contributed $2,000 for the erection of a tent in order that the services might be carried on throughout the summer months."

The fact that his congregation raised $2,000.00 for the tent during the early weeks of June is interesting, especially when you consider that just five months earlier he spoke to only 24 dispirited members at the opening service.

Because of climatic limitations, the tent had a short life. Knowing that it would be a backward step to return to The Parkdale Tabernacle, Smith began plugging for a new and enlarged work. He argued that you couldn't deny the fact that he had not only consolidated the Bosworth results, he had improved upon them. He also had, in effect, put the Christian and Missionary Alliance denomination in a prime position, at least in Toronto. No one argued that he hadn't and with the support of the denomination and his congregation, plans were made to build a new and impressive church. Every facet of the work was considered and the new structure was designed to accommodate the existing demands and provide scope for future growth.

It's one thing to announce an ambitious building program, it's another thing to finance it.

Smith's major claim to religious fame has been his ability to raise vast sums of money for missionary programs. He has devised and evolved a technique which has resulted in the raising of well over twelve million dollars for his one passion . . . foreign missions.

His experience with fund-raising for the new church took a different twist. It was done in a manner which he has never repeated or duplicated since.

"Little by little the money came in," he recalls. "We were given a $1,000.00 Victory Bond. Someone offered us a check for the building fund or a house for a manse. We took the former. Another interested party gave a Victory Bond for a car. We accepted it on the condition that it go into the fund instead of toward a car. A short time later a Mr. W. A. Conkin gave us a new car. The largest single donation came after the entire congregation spent a half-day in intercessory prayer for the new work. Mr. George R. Gregg placed $15,000.00 at the disposal of the building committee.

"We were elated by the response and generosity of the congregation. Besides large gifts of up to $5,000.00 there were many from just a few cents to hundreds of dollars. The site we picked for the church was on Christie Street overlooking

Willowvale Park in Toronto's mid-western area. It was right on the Bloor Street car line and offered easy access to and from all parts of the city.

"The building was not intended to be a magnificent edifice reaching up to the skies. Rather, it was a functional building designed primarily as a spiritual workshop. It was 80 feet wide and 130 feet long and cost $40,000, including furnishing. There wasn't any provision for Sunday school or young peoples' facilities. It was just a large, plain auditorium with a seating capacity of 1,800. The only additions to the main auditorium were a small pastor's study, a choir loft and bookroom."

The dedication services were held on Sunday, May 14, 1922, and once again Paul Rader was the guest speaker. During the services an offering was taken up in the form of cash and pledges. When the total was announced the congregation could hardly believe its ears. Just over $5,000.00 was raised for the furtherance of the work. This came right on the heels of a concentrated year of fund-raising by the new church.

Called The Alliance Tabernacle, it was Oswald Smith's second major ministry in the city of Toronto. Its success solidified his reputation as an outstanding preacher and he became one of the city's most talked-about clerics.

For the next six years Smith and his church on Christie Street prospered both materially and spiritually. Never one to place much emphasis on material possessions, he was, nevertheless, able to devote his energies wholly to the running of the church because the worry of personal comforts and finances no longer vied for his attention. He was making a satisfactory salary and, as a result, provided for his wife and three children in a modest but comfortable manner.

The church grew in numbers and influence. Never forgetting the lessons he learned from the Bosworth Brothers, he packed the auditorium night after night by giving the people something they could not get at any other church in the city . . . variety.

Realizing that he could not hope to hold the interest with

135

his preaching alone, he brought in guest speakers, one after the other. He also appealed to the younger crowd and those who go to church simply for the music. He was the first minister in Toronto to bring in the world-renowned Cleveland Colored Quintet. Their particular brand of Gospel singing caught the imagination of the people and they were in constant demand. Featured speakers were all high caliber: men such as the Negro evangelist, Charles Morris, from Virginia; John Paul, D.D. who was President of Taylor University, Upland, Indiana; and Dr. H. C. Morrison, President of Asbury Seminary, Wilmore, Kentucky. It was not uncommon, especially in the summer months, for those who couldn't get seats to crowd around the open windows and follow the service from outside.

There are two definite schools of thought as to the best method of retaining a congregation's interest. Many advocate the advantages of a constant ministry where the members become accustomed to seeing the same face in the pulpit Sunday after Sunday. They argue that this creates an empathy between the parishioner and the minister. One always knows where the other will be. It creates a comfortable atmosphere, somewhat like an old pair of shoes.

The other school of thought is always to maintain an air of the unexpected. This is the approach that Smith has followed through the years. He reasoned that by bringing in a constant stream of speakers it strengthened his own ministry. Instead of being taken for granted, the congregation took notice of what he had to say. They looked forward to his appearance in the pulpit and he responded to their enthusiasm.

Smith's thoughts along this line are very candid: "It simply boils down to keeping fresh. It's just as bad for me to become stale as it is for the congregation to become stale for me. I'm sure that they welcomed a new face in the pulpit just as much as I welcomed the stimulation of preaching to a completely new audience. Besides, it gave me the opportunity to travel and as a result I was able to keep my messages current and topical."

Bruce Fogerty, a prominent Toronto real estate executive who first started attending Smith's church in the early 30's, has remained down through the years to become a member of the Board of Managers, teacher of the Adult Bible Class, and close personal friend.

"I have never quarreled with his approach in this matter," said Fogerty. "In fact, the very opposite is true. One thing that attracted me to his church in the first place was the freshness of the services and the excitement of hearing some of the best preachers and musicians in the business. I've always held, and I know that I speak for the Board in this case, that Dr. Smith is a world figure, and as such the church has become a world church. To limit him to a routine ministry would be to limit the church. Instead of losing, we have been the beneficiaries in this instance. How else could we have ever heard evangelists such as Gypsy Smith or Bible teachers of the caliber of Dr. Walter Wilson, Dr. Harry Ironside, or Dr. Graham Scroggie? If we had been saddled with a man who guarded his pulpit so jealously that he wouldn't allow anyone to take his place just in case they were better than he might be, we'd have had a pretty dull church.

"Dr. Smith would probably be the first to agree that many of the guest speakers were more eloquent than he ever was. I honestly don't think he ever gave it the slightest thought. All he wanted for his congregation was the very best. This resulted in the congregation looking forward to his every message. I've never known him to bomb, as it were. Regardless of what he was preaching about, he was always able to draw upon some experience he received during his travels. We as a congregation have been the fortunate ones. When he was in complete charge of the work there was none better. When he went away the best replaced him and when he returned everyone flocked to hear what he had to say. What minister could ask for anything more?"

This freedom to travel has resulted in making Smith one of the most traveled evangelical leaders in Canada and North America.

The Alliance Tabernacle and its people exerted a direct

influence on the community. Not only did the church remain open practically every night as crowds flocked to the services, it moved out into the streets in public demonstrations.

The Evening Telegram ran a four column picture in the evening edition on Monday, October 19, 1925. The picture showed a long line of people holding placards which stretched into infinity. The messages on the cards highlighted one main theme: "The Lord Is at Hand"; "Christ Is Coming Again" and "Be Ready to Meet Thy God." This was the Clark and Bell Campaign.

The caption under the picture read, "More than one thousand men and women took part in the parade, held on Saturday afternoon from the Alliance Tabernacle, Christie Street. The banners carried emphasized the second coming and inscriptions exhorted people to seek the new birth and be in a state of preparedness for the great event."

The work was also branching out internationally as well. Smith emphasized missions and generated a deep-seated interest in this basically new subject for many in his congregation. His people responded in magnificent style. Considering that for many, the word missions merely meant some place that serves soup and salvation to the "down-and-outers," they caught the vision quickly. It is safe to say that Smith has hardly preached a sermon during which he did not make some reference to the needs of the foreign fields. Their response is reflected in the missionary offerings received during the first six years of the Alliance's operation: $3,593.00; $5,630.00; $10,323.00; $16,756.00; $22,795.00; and $34,000.00. This totaled $94,195 in less time than it takes many new churches to really get consolidated.

One reason might have been Smith's philosophy as far as church debts are concerned.

"No long-term mortage was ever placed on the Tabernacle. The first payment fell due on October 16, 1922. Following two half nights of earnest prayer by the faithful in the congregation, a cash offering was taken which totaled just over $3,100.00. This more than covered the principal and interest. The final payment, which amounted to $3,743.00, was due six months later. I reminded the congregation of our indebtedness and my desire to clear the church off so that we could channel everything into the proclamation of the Gospel. I prayed that God would undertake and He did. The offering was taken on the Sunday preceding the payment date and His people gave $4,090.70 in cash, plus additional 30-day pledges for $759.00. This meant that we wiped the entire debt off and had nearly $1,100.00 left over. It was a wonderful day."

Because of the financial freedom which came from a debt-free environment, the Tabernacle formed a number of groups and organizations. These made significant contributions in the field of witnessing and proclaiming the Gospel.

THE TABERNACLE PUBLISHERS: this organization sold thousands of dollars worth of religious books.

THE WAYSIDE MISSION: sent workers out two-by-two to preach and minister in the Canadian northland.

THE PROPHET (which was later to become *The Peoples Magazine*): was a monthly magazine published by the Tabernacle.

THE KING'S MESSENGERS: a band of tract distributors who handed out nearly 100,000 tracts the first year they were in operation.

HOUSE OF SEEKERS AFTER TRUTH: organized to provide a place where Jewish people could come for guidance and instruction. It was under the direction of an ex-Rabbi, Henry Bregman.

Smith has never been one to hold back and not give his full attention or energies to the work. There has never been any question of which comes first in his life. He has always reasoned that by involving as many as possible there is much less chance of losing them. If they are taking an active role in the church they will take more interest. In the case of the tabernacle this philosophy paid off.

As the Tabernacle's influence and reputation grew, so did Smith's. Soon he was receiving calls from various parts of the United States. He was in demand as a speaker and convention leader. Feeling confident that he had the church on a solid footing and knowing that it was with the full approval of his board and congregation, he began to accept appointments. These engagements sometimes took the form of official calls to other pulpits. He was extremely flattered that The Gospel Tabernacle of New York considered him seriously as a replacement for A. B. Simpson, the founder of the Christian and Missionary Alliance. It was even more flattering that "the mother church of the Alliance," as it was called, would even consider a 33-year-old Canadian minister in the first place. Tempting as the offer was, he turned it down to stay in Toronto, where he felt God had called him.

The months of 1923 and 1924 were busy ones for Smith. He was solidly booked and had reached the enviable position of being able to select and reject invitations. As the demand for his time increased, so did the standing of those inviting him. Some of the largest and most influential churches in Canada and the United States began looking upon Smith favorably and vied for openings in his schedule.

One of the guest evangelists Smith brought to The Alliance Tabernacle was William Fetler, the Founder and General Director of the Russian Missionary Society. This man's burning passion was to reach the Russians with the Gospel. His picturesque eloquence caught the imagination of the congregation and especially Smith. Fetler made the point that those of Russian origin who were living in the Baltic countries, such as Lithuania, Latvia and Poland, were ripe for evangelism. He based his argument on the fact that they were living in predominantly Roman and Greek Catholic countries and would be receptive to Protestant evangelizing.

Smith was sold on the idea and for weeks talked of nothing else. By early summer Fetler had completed the necessary arrangements for an extended tour with Smith as the featured speaker.

On July 2, 1924, Smith set sail from Quebec City on the *Empress of Scotland* for his evangelistic crusade with the Russians of Europe. Fetler had gone ahead to make the necessary arrangements.

For the next two months Smith and Fetler traveled through

the Baltic countries preaching to the Russian people in their own tongue. Many of the auditoriums seated over 2,000 and they were generally packed with every seat taken. The walls were usually lined with eager listeners. Smith became quite proficient in the art of preaching through interpretation. He was in later years to be the one who introduced this style of ministry to Billy Graham and to teach him its finer points.

"We held services in the Latvian cities of Riga, Libau, and Mitau. The people were more than responsive, they were frighteningly receptive. They seemed to have a hunger for God's Word. From Latvia we moved on to Poland, which is one of the most fascinating countries in that area. Services were conducted in many small towns and villages. By the time we finally reached Warsaw my stomach was acting up and I was taken severely ill. I suppose it was the strange diet but I can't remember ever having felt so absolutely miserable before or since in my life. Thankfully, it only lasted a short time and after a good rest I was ready to continue my heavy preaching schedule. In addition to the Russian-speaking community I preached to the German residents of Poland. They were also a responsive group. I was told that in the first five years following the First World War between 4,000 and 5,000 Germans in the area had made decisions for Christ. A least 2,000 were baptized believers. The response was unbelievable. All I had to do was start the invitation and before I was very far along they would stream forward seeking salvation. I've often looked back on those experiences when I've preached in Canada and the United States and the people have been difficult to move."

In addition to the Baltic countries Smith traveled through England, Holland, France, Switzerland, Lithuania and Luxemburg. While he didn't spend much time in any one place, or country, the little he saw opened his eyes to the world at large. This was his field and the beginning of his major role as a missionary zealot.

His return to Toronto and The Alliance Tabernacle was a triumph. He was a celebrity, one who in the days of limited travel had "seen the world." Crowds flocked to hear what he had to say. He inspired the people for missions as he himself was fired up. For the next two years The Tabernacle rode on a wave of perennial revival. Campaign followed campaign and the people hardly had time to recover from one series of meetings until they were right in the midst of another.

The Tabernacle had become tagged "Toronto's Great Center of Evangelism" and so great were the crowds that the building had to be enlarged on two occasions. The seating capacity finally totaled 2,000 and still there were numerous occasions when well over 1,000 were turned away from the services. It was a time of blessing for both Smith and his people. Scores came forward every time the invitation was given, which was following every evangelistic meeting.

"I've never relied on instinct to give an invitation, as some men do," said Smith. "I feel that the best way to get people saved is to get them forward. The only way to get them forward is to get them on their feet and moving. I know that God can work in the pews. He also works in the counseling room where the ones coming forward have the advantage of talking to trained personal workers. Their chances are a lot better under those circumstances. I think it is the evangelist's responsibility to give those who are being moved by the Holy Spirit every advantage. Nothing beats an invitation where someone steps forward. It's an experience they never forget."

Smith pioneered soul-winning in Toronto. No other church up to that time had ever conducted evangelistic meetings with such intensity. Complementing the crusades was a new innovation . . . the gospel song. The bane of many ministers who were honestly attempting to reach the lost was the music they were using. It was a throwback to the Victorian style of hymn which lacked spirit and enthusiasm. The Cleveland Quintet's success was mainly in its spirited, happy music, which became infectious. Smith was fortunate in having as his soloist and song leader, Fred L. Syme. As has been the case with all of Smith's musical directors, this man was a master in the art of leading congregational singing. Smith has always placed great value in music as a mood-setter for his preaching. There were many good, lively songs written during and prior to that period, but they were never used to any extent in Toronto until

Smith introduced them in his meetings. It wasn't too long until the people were singing such old favorites as: "More About Jesus"; "I'll Go Where You Want Me to Go"; "Lead Me to Calvary"; "When We All Get to Heaven" and Charles H. Gabriel's classic, "Oh, That Will Be Glory." He still used the time-honored hymns of the church such as: Wesley's "Jesus, Lover of My Soul"; Newton's "Glorious Things of Thee Are Spoken" and Whiting's "Eternal Father Strong to Save" during the Sunday morning worship services.

Smith fully appreciated the value of a balanced program for the church and accepted the fact that it couldn't survive solely on evangelism. He attempted to walk a tight line between Bible teaching, evangelism and missions. Unfortunately, he was not sufficiently adaptable at dealing with thought-leaders within the group. Every church has some who exert their positive ideas on others and become the motivators of unrest. Success at dealing with people such as this and the situations which arise only comes from years of experience.

"I always believed that if the church was to grow, hold its young people and reproduce, it must emphasize evangelism. The church that doesn't evangelize will fossilize and all you have to do is look around at the churches of today to see that this is true," said Smith in explaining what happened at The Alliance Tabernacle. "There are many churches which stress Bible teaching, and I thank God for them because it is so very necessary, but they do not grow. I tried to offset our evangelistic services on Sunday by setting Wednesday and Friday nights aside for Bible exposition.

The Alliance was very anxious for Smith to head up their work in Canada but this would necessitate his resignation as pastor.

"After much prayer and many heartaches," said Smith, "I finally decided to accept the position of Superintendent for Canada."

His resignation took place on June 20, 1926.

For the next few months it was one church after the other as he filled speaking engagements in Ontario, Georgia, Florida and Texas. The meetings were successful and he enjoyed the release from pastoral responsibilities. It was nearly a year later, April 10, 1927, that he accepted a call to become minister of The Gospel Tabernacle in Los Angeles, California. It was another Christian and Missionary Alliance church and he felt that he was ready once more to take over such a work. Los Angeles appealed to him when he was first approached as he thought the complete change would be beneficial both physically and spiritually. He had hardly been there a week when he realized that Toronto was where he really belonged and the vision he had in British Columbia was still valid.

The Gospel Tabernacle was a well-equipped building with an auditorium seating 1,200. At first there were less than 200 in the congregation, but before long Smith was preaching to filled pews. California was a mecca, and still is, for religious fanatics and cults, and part of Smith's success can probably be attributed to his straightforward preaching and imaginative programming techniques.

Wanting to reach the entire city of Los Angeles instead of just being confined to an area, he persuaded his board members to let him lease Trinity Auditorium in downtown Los Angeles for Sunday afternoon services. He was sure he could fill it and his arguments convinced the board.

"I was fortunate in having as my musical director, Mr. S. E. Ramseyer, who built up a superb choir and orchestra. Included in the choir were a number of well-trained voices and the quality of the music drew the people. R. G. LeTourneau and his wife were in the choir and it was there that I began my association and friendship with this great American industrialist. His success in the design and manufacture of heavy earth-moving equipment has made him a millionaire many times over. Despite all his fame and money he has always been an avid supporter of world missions and a man of God.

"I opened in Trinity Auditorium by preaching a series of prophetic messages which I entitled 'The Second Coming of Christ, The Only Hope of the World.' I knew that, especially in California, people had an intense interest in the future and they would come to hear me. I was right. Pretty soon we had to bring in extra chairs, because the 2,200 seats were quickly filled for each meeting." He was 37 years old.

Delighted that he was a success and that the Lord was blessing, Smith nevertheless was restless and could not get Toronto and his ultimate calling out of his mind.

He was comfortably settled with his family in Los Angeles and outwardly appeared to be content. One of the highlights of the ministry was his participation in a campaign for funds to help William Fetler complete a tabernacle for the Russian work in Riga, Latvia. Together with Reverend Michael Billester, a Russian American, and Madam Maria Karinskaya, a famed Russian prima-donna, he helped to raise $10,000.00 for Fetler's work.

Even though his church board pleaded with him, and a group of men offered to build a 3,000 seat tabernacle if he remained, Smith resigned his pastorate. He preached his farewell sermon on April 1, 1928, to a saddened congregation. After settling up his personal affairs he left by car for Toronto, with Daisy, the three children, and Chrissie French, who had joined the Smith household prior to the move to California. She was maid, nurse, cook, mother-confessor and general factotum. In addition to all this she was idolized by the children, adored by Daisy and for Oswald, indispensable!

Daisy remembers the trip with a shudder. "It was the worst experience I've ever been through. We left on May 16 and it took us twelve days to cover the 3,000 miles. I think I counted every bump on the gravel roads. There weren't many paved ones in those days. To make matters worse Hope came down with the mumps and the car, which was a brand new Nash, acted up. It was a series of tire and engine breakdowns all along the way. I was determined that that would be the last time I ever traveled with children. By the time we reached Toronto, Oswald wasn't giving me any arguments. I was fortunate that we had Chrissie along to help because I don't know how I'd ever have managed all by myself."

Smith returned to Toronto with absolutely nothing in sight. His only comfort were the dozen or so faithful followers who met regularly for prayer following his return and pleaded with God to open up a new work for their pastor in Toronto.

The Alliance Tabernacle of Toronto

Paul Smith, "the golden-voiced soloist," at the age of 5

Chapter 13

It is an accepted historical fact that most religious movements flourished during times of severe economic or social upheaval.

The Mormons of the United States and the Pilgrims of England are two excellent examples. Their greatest achievements and influence came under stress and privation.

During the two World Wars, for example, everyone became aware of God. Many who had never given church or religion a thought were suddenly turning to spiritual matters. Another period of history when the entire nation was conscious of God was during the "Great Depression" of the '30's. People had little else to take their minds off the drab economic level to which the nation had slipped. Church became their spiritual comfort, emotional outlet and entertainment. This was the time a number of the existing churches consolidated and personal careers hit their peak. People went to church mainly because it was free. There just wasn't any money to spare for recreation or personal pleasures. Church attendance hit an all-time high during those years, and it has never been equaled before or since.

On Friday, November 1, 1929, the stock markets of North America opened with optimism but before they closed, fortunes were lost. Financiers all over the world stood by helplessly as their empires collapsed in the crash of "Black Friday."

It might be considered coincidental, but it was just fourteen months previous to the national disaster that Oswald Smith launched his final and certainly greatest work. By the time the nation had begun to stagger out from under its shock and settle into a decade of the worst depression in history, Smith had an established church and was reaping the benefits of an upsurge in religious interest.

Following his return from Los Angeles he spent another period of undecision. Lesser men would have given up on Toronto and taken the course of least resistance. Many would have been content with a quiet, well-paying pastorate which took a minimum of attention and effort. This was not Smith's idea of the ministry. He never purposely looked for the easy way out. The opposite was usually true.

"As I look back over the years," he recalled, "I can see where I could have been easier on myself, and those around me, if I had been what some people termed flexible. It was not in my make-up to consider the alternatives. Instead, I knew what God would have me to do and went ahead. It's unfortunate that in so doing I might have ruffled some people, but generally I feel confident that the end justified my means. In any case, I have a certain satisfaction in knowing that if I had been always thinking about this one or that one I'd have spent more time on personalities than getting on with the job. The founding and establishing of The Peoples Church is a good example.

"I always had the vision of British Columbia in my mind and could not accept the fact that God might have made a mistake. I could have stayed in Los Angeles and probably still have been there with a very successful work. But I would have never been satisfied. I've sometimes been asked how I could give up the security of a pastorate, such as I had in California, and return to Toronto with absolutely nothing ahead of me? My answer is, that if I had thought about it, I'd probably been scared half to death and never made the move. As it was, I knew I wasn't in the right place, but security and material things were secondary. I wanted to serve God and serve Him in the place He would have me. It's that simple."

It may have been simple in theory. In actuality, it was hard work with many disappointments before his dream became a reality.

In the past, Smith's other two major works were started under different conditions. Dale was an established church and The Alliance Tabernacle grew like "Topsy." This time, Smith decided, the work would begin at the top instead of at the bottom.

"Massey Hall was Toronto's largest public auditorium, and I was quite familiar with what it would take to fill it.

"Chapman and Alexander had an efficient organization backing them up and the Bosworth Brothers had a whole denomination supporting their efforts. I had nothing except a burning desire to get my church established. Fortunately, there was a small nucleus of faithful followers from my previous works who encouraged me with their prayers and modest support. I shudder to think about it now because I could easily have finished my whole career right on the platform of Massey Hall. Thankfully, I didn't have the time or energy to worry about such eventualities."

Smith has often pointed out that if he had started his church as he did The Gospel Auditorium, it would have taken years to build up . . . but he didn't have time to wait.

Soon after his return from California he accepted Paul Rader's invitation to join the Worldwide Christian Couriers. Rader was President and appointed Smith Director of Canada with the commission to organize a soul-winning work in Toronto. Rader offered his full support and assistance. Also contributing to the proposed program was Clinton H. Churchhill, who had established The Churchill Tabernacle in Buffalo, New York, and enjoyed an extended ministry as one of New York State's leading evangelical ministers.

On September 9, 1928, Smith held his first service in Massey Hall. As he walked out onto the platform and faced an audience of nearly 2,000 people he could not help but remember the countless meetings he had attended when men such as Torrey, Chapman, Alexander, and Gypsy Smith preached the Word of God as he was now about to do.

"I couldn't help wondering if they felt as I did. I'm sure they didn't because they were well promoted and had a guaranteed audience. I'm positive they prayed before they walked through the door at the side of the platform. I'll tell you one thing, they didn't pray any more fervently than I did that Sunday evening."

The first meeting went off better than he had believed possible. The people seemed to respond to his brand of preaching. The Cosmopolitan Tabernacle was born on the stage of Massey Hall. Each succeeding Sunday night saw the crowds improve and the response to the invitation grow meeting by meeting.

For the next four months, until January 13, 1929, Sunday evening services of The Tabernacle were held in Massey Hall. Before many meetings the auditorium was completely filled right up to the second balcony. The end came on the 13th when Smith preached his farewell message. He was leaving once again for Europe and his second mission to the Russian-speaking people in the Baltic countries. This time it was at the invitation of Rader who recognized in Smith, the potential of a missionary leader.

His itinerary was significantly more extensive than in 1924. This time he visited England, France, Belgium, Monaco, Italy, Austria, Germany, Latvia, Lithuania, Estonia, Spain, Poland and Switzerland.

Instead of just preaching and evangelizing, Smith's efforts were channelled into concrete results. All the time he was ministering he was paying close attention to the needs of the various fields and making careful notes. Upon his return these notes were turned into a detailed report for Rader with definite recommendations which were accepted in total and acted upon. As a result of his trip a Bible school was established in Riga, Latvia, for the expressed purpose of training national missionaries. Their success at evangelizing their own people proved to Smith the value of using nationals to reach nationals. This lesson was to be remembered in later years when foreign missionaries of British, Canadian and American origin were forced out of countries because of political pressures.

In addition to the Baltic countries Smith was instrumental in establishing and encouraging a concentrated work among the refugees of France and Belgium. These people, who were the victims of wars and oppressions in their own countries, were merely tolerated by the host nation. As a result, the missionaries were given practically a free hand because they also ministered in a practical manner as well as spiritual. The final highlight of his tour was the establishment of a Bible School in predominantly Roman Catholic Spain. This was only possible because the stringent conditions of the Spanish Government were met. It also had to be proven that the school would benefit the Spanish people. Not only was a school established, but permission was granted for an American missionary to come out from the United States and become dean.

For the next ten years the Couriers and Smith's congregation supported about forty full-time national workers on the mission fields of Spain, France, Belgium and Latvia. In Latvia, especially, the success was outstanding as 2,000 were converted.

It was during this trip that Smith first heard one of his hymns sung in a foreign language.

"It was at Riga that they sang 'Saved' in the Latvian language. It was a great thrill for me personally. The congregation numbered well over 1,300. The Latvian word for saved was *glabts* and surprisingly enough it fitted right into the meter of the music and sounded perfectly natural."

His return home was a triumph, not only for him personally but for his faithful congregation who once again took up where they had left off in Massey Hall five months before. They packed out the building to welcome him home and launch the first Courier Missionary Convention. Smith preached as he had never preached before. The trip had given a new vitality to his ministry. Almost as much to his surprise, as Rader's, just over $10,000.00 was raised for foreign missions during the three-day conference which ran from June 27th to 30th. For the next six months Smith moved about the United States preaching on behalf of the Couriers. During that period he succeeded in personally raising cash and faith promise missionary offerings in excess of $60,000.00.

He was now an active missionary promoter and as such, well on his way to becoming a world traveler.

As his stature grew with the Couriers and the churches he visited so did his family in Toronto. True as her word, Daisy stayed at home raising the children as her husband moved about from place to place exhorting the people on behalf of missions.

"I was content to let Oswald go wherever the Lord led," said his wife. "I felt that God had called him and it was a great opportunity. I never stood in his way because I always considered my place was in the home while the children were growing up. We were both in full agreement on this matter."

His daughter Hope saw her father through the eyes of a child during those early years of his travels. "We never knew anything else. He used to be home for a while then leave. It was our way of life. He would write short letters to me and I enjoyed receiving them. Mother and Chrissie were always there and this gave us kids a sense of security. Occasionally he brought back presents someone gave him for us children."

On March 30, 1930, Smith made yet another move. This time it was from Massey Hall to a more permanent location. For some time three dedicated laymen, A. G. Ward, Sydney Perkins and Edward Day, had been struggling to carry on an evangelistic work in the empty St. James Square Presbyterian

Church on Gerrard Street East. The building became vacant following the union of the Presbyterian and Methodist Churches into the United Church of Canada. Ambitious and commendable though their plans may have been, the men just didn't have enough experience or ability to make the work a success. They attempted to draw crowds with special speakers and musical talent. To their credit they managed to work up a respectable congregation of between 500 and 700 in a building seating upwards of 1,500. It was, however, not enough to offset the heavy expenses of such an endeavor. There was rent, honorariums, traveling and accommodation expenses for the speakers and talent who were brought in from as far away as the United States and Great Britain.

The men were about at their wits' end when their musical director, Eldon B. Lehman, suggested that they try to get someone to take over the work. They jumped at the idea and began to look about. Lehman could see why they were having problems and recommended a man who could sell the people on a continuous program and was also strong enough to carry the entire work on his own. Just such a man, in his opinion, was Oswald J. Smith who was immediately contacted by Day.

"I had never held a conversation with Smith up to that point," recalls Lehman. "I'd heard about him and for some reason, when the decision got around to unloading the work, his name came to mind. I really wasn't too interested because I had made up my mind to quit anyway. It seemed pointless to continue when you never knew for sure if there would even be another meeting.

"I remember the first time I really met Smith. He was invited by the men to come and speak and look over the situation. We publicized his appearance in the church and over the radio and the place was packed. It was a great Sunday morning service. We were scheduled to broadcast our radio program that afternoon at five and Smith came to see what we were doing. Following the broadcast I called for attention and told my choir and small band that this was my last service. I said it had been a good time and I was sorry to have to end it. I was just about to continue when Smith jumped up and rushed forward from where he was sitting at the rear of the room. 'I won't let you do it. I won't take over the work unless you stay on.'

"I was completely flabbergasted. I'd never even thought about working with him. As far as I knew he didn't even know a thing about me. That was the beginning and, for me, the start of something which I shall always cherish as one of the most rewarding periods of my life."

Smith also remembers the occasion, "I knew the moment I saw the man on the platform that he was good, real good. His ability at molding an audience into a giant choir has, in my opinion, never been equaled. There have been leaders with more technical ability and musical experience but none better with a congregation. I knew that if I was to make a go of the work I had to have Lehman as my director of music. I've always been thankful that he accepted without hesitation."

Smith moved his established congregation from Massey Hall and it amalgamated into the one formed by Ward, Perkins and Day. The three men were relieved to be freed of the responsibility and thankful that someone was continuing the work they had started.

Before too long, a solid evangelical church was flourishing. Smith was in complete charge of both the platform and radio program. Together with Lehman, he began building the congregation until it was soon straining the facilities of the auditorium.

Since he was no longer bound by denominational restrictions, he was able to implement many of his own ideas and know that there wouldn't be open opposition. He eliminated membership interference by not creating a voting membership. Instead, he appointed a Board of Managers comprised of sound Christian men. To these men and these alone he answered. Instead of creating a board of "yes" men, he carefully and prayerfully gathered together men of strong convictions who through their own personalities exerted restraints whenever they deemed it necessary. Such occasions were rare since they were in full agreement with the concepts of the program and as a result it was a harmonious relationship. This complete understanding and mutual respect has continued down through the years. The board and minister of The Peoples Church now function as a team.

Such an environment was what Smith wanted, because he had been through years of democratic memberships and felt that it severely limited his particular approach to preaching the Gospel. The result of such a form of church government was an unbroken period of harmony without splits or schisms. If someone differed it was their privilege to leave and worship in a communion where they have a vote and say in church affairs. It is generally accepted by those who have been with Smith down through the years that such occurrences were minor in number when compared to the hundreds who have been faithful adherents.

The secret of his ability in holding a congregation week after week was in the basic lessons he learned from the Bosworths. He knew that during the depression years the people would come and keep coming if a steady diet of campaigns was offered with different speakers and musicians. He gave them what they wanted and his schedule for 1931 emphasized his strong convictions in this area:

1931

March 25 to April 8	Jubilee Colored Quartette
April 12 to April 26	Dr. Arthur Brown
May 3 to May 15	Newton N. Riddell
May 17 to May 31	Rev. Paul Rader
June 1 to June 7	Annual Missionary Convention
June 11 to June 14	Robert Harkness
June 14 to June 28	Rev. Dean C. Dutton, D.D.
July 5 to July 19	Rev. J. C. Kellogg
July 26 to August 9	Rev. John W. Robertson
August 16 to September 2	Rev. A. P. Gouthey, D.D.
September 6 to September 20	Rev. Andrew Johnson, D.D., PH.D.
September 27 to October 7	Rev. F. Lincicome
September 27 to October 7	Jubilee Singers
October 11 to October 25	Rev. Gerald B. Winrod
November 1 to November 15	Rev. Wm. B. Hogg, D.D.

Backing up these special attractions was Lehman with his choir and musicians. With his special talent for attracting high caliber people, Lehman, within a very short time, had amassed a choir of around 100 voices and a full orchestra which, on special occasions numbered over 50 players. Lehman's reputation as a musician and Smith's as a minister drew people from all over the city. It was not uncommon for Lehman to be directing as many as seven gold medalists in his orchestra.

Paul Smith was one of Lehman's musicians: "I consider Eldon Lehman to have been tops in his field. He was in a class by himself for the years he was connected with the church and my father. He established the musical foundations for The Peoples Church and they are still evident today. We have up-dated our approach but the basics are Lehman's and probably always will be. He served the people the kind of music they could identify with and in return, they allowed themselves to be led by this gifted man, in a manner that is rare in gospel music."

In spite of his unqualified success, Smith still had a gnawing unrest. He couldn't get The Alliance Tabernacle out of his mind. It rankled him that somewhere he had failed it or it had failed him. Many months passed before he finally got it out of his system and began to look at the Toronto Gospel Tabernacle as his prime work in the City of Toronto. He was now sure that Dale and Alliance were secondary and this present work was what God had planned for him, from the time he went forward in Massey Hall to give his life for full-time service.

By the fall of 1933 he was completely settled into his pastorate and enjoying absolute freedom. This was something he had never experienced before in any of his other churches. His preaching and overall ministry reflected this new attitude . . . so did the results as the counseling room was filled following every invitation.

His congregation was loyal and never questioned his approach to preaching or programs which brought in some of the best men of the day. He relied upon his board to look after the administrative duties but at the same time he kept a close watch on the entire operation. Because he was surrounded with competent and dedicated men he was able to maintain a constant program of global trips on behalf of missions and evangelism.

Realizing that someone had to be left in charge while he was away he persuaded Lehman to quit his job with a wholesale grocery firm and become office manager and chief accountant. So complete was his trust and confidence in this man that he turned the church over to him on numerous occasions for extended periods of up to three to five months and never worried about what would happen. To his credit Lehman was the perfect associate, and whenever Smith would return it was always to an enthusiastic congregation which had been well treated and served during his absence.

For Lehman it was an ideal arrangement. "Smith would set the basic program before he left. We'd go over who was coming and the dates would be established. After that everything was left up to me.

"I remember one time, early during our association, when he went away on a trip and I asked the congregation for volunteers to form an orchestra. The response was fantastic. They came from all over and I never told Smith about it until he came on the platform and heard the full orchestra play. He couldn't speak."

On October 1, 1933, Smith made an announcement in the church which surprised and at the same time pleased his congregation.

"I had been thinking and praying about this problem for many months. I had always felt that perhaps some of my failure at Alliance was because I was confined by denominational bounds. I never really felt free to reach out and try to interest those in other churches because it is an unwritten law which says that one denomination does not 'sheep steal' from another. I had no intention of stealing, yet at the same time, I honestly felt that I had something to offer those who might be tired or disappointed with what they were getting. Sometimes the only thing which holds a person from leaving one church for another is changing denominations. It can also be a drawback for those who do not want to become identified as one thing or another. They just want to be Christians worshiping in a Bible-believing church. Recalling my vision in British Columbia and the vivid picture of preaching to all the people of Toronto I decided this is what I would call my church . . . The Peoples Church."

One of the side effects of the "Union" of the Methodist and Presbyterian Churches was the number of congregations which either amalgamated or completely disappeared from existence. One of these was the Central Methodist Church. It was a large, well equipped building of Italian architecture with cushioned pews. Smith would pass by it on his way to Gerrard Street and think about the waste of such a building in what had to be the prime location for a cosmopolitan church. The more he thought about it and the 2,000 empty seats, the more determined he became to get it. Following meetings with the owners and long discussions with his Board of Managers the arrangements were completed and The Peoples Church changed its address to 100 Bloor Street East, an address which was to become as well known as the church itself. The date of the move was July 1, 1934.

The Peoples Church, 100 Bloor St., in Toronto

Chapter 14

The move to Bloor Street crystallized Smith's ministry in the city of Toronto and the world, for that matter. Up to this point he was just a moderately successful minister who had gained a certain amount of attention from both secular and religious interests. With the move, he became a man of singular importance. No longer was he a denominationalist who represented a specific point of view . . . he was an individualist, and as such, represented the largest single Protestant congregation in the Dominion of Canada. What he said was news, what he did, was news, and who he brought into his pulpit was news.

This attention from the press is evident by the bulging scrapbook Smith has maintained over the years. Most of his press is good, but some of it caused him many sleepless nights. It all began shortly after the purchase of the property at 100 Bloor Street East.

"From as early as 1930," said Smith, "my congregation had urged me to buy or build my own church, but I refused because I didn't want to go into debt. Even on Gerrard Street they were constantly pressuring me. I suppose it was an unconscious desire to belong to a real church instead of just a rented building. I really didn't blame them because I wanted something permanent just as badly as they did.

"I had always felt that I would leave the church in a real fix if I happened to die before a debt was paid off. I never liked owing money for anything, even a church. I had the memory of the men who started the work on Gerrard Street in my mind and was determined that no congregation of mine would ever be saddled with impossible financial burdens after I was gone, especially burdens which I had created.

"Their arguments were pretty good. It was pointed out to me, in no uncertain terms, that with a congregation of over 3,000 adherents it wouldn't be too hard to raise the necessary money. It was a hard position to defend. I prayed about it for some time and finally announced during the radio broadcast of a service that I'd buy a permanent building for The Peoples Church if someone would first give me a gift of $10,000.00. The people laughed at the suggestion and I couldn't blame them because it did seem outrageous. The country was in the midst of a bitter depression and money was scarce. I might as well ask for the moon while I was at it, I was told.

"Some thought I'd lost my faith in God and what He could do by making my demands so steep. I countered with the statement that if He wanted us to have the money, He'd send it in. It's just as simple as that.

"The matter was shelved and for the next six years we paid rent and built up the work and by 1936 we were, I believe, at the apex of our success and influence. This peak was maintained for many years. When I say we were at our apex I mean that everything was a success. The meetings were outstanding, the congregations magnificent and the results unbelievable. That evaluation of the work may seem boastful, but it is the only honest and adequate manner in which I can describe what it was like during those wonderful years."

Smith's wife was directly involved with the circumstances which led up to his purchasing the church. She remembers exactly what happened:

"Oswald and I were invited to have dinner with Mr. William G. Jaffray and his wife. He was the publisher and owner of *The Globe*. Mr. Jaffray had always been sympathetic toward The Peoples Church. His paper reported many of the major news happenings fairly and without bias.

"During dinner, the conversation got around to the possible purchase of a building for the church. Oswald blurted out that he'd been offered the opportunity to purchase 100

160

Bloor Street for $65,000.00 but wouldn't commit himself unless someone gave him an outright gift for at least one-third of the total price.

"I thought he was stark raving mad and told him so. I had honestly expected him to come up with something like $5,000.00 not a third of $65,000.00.

"The next morning, after Oswald had left for the church, I got a telephone call from Mr. Jaffray. He asked me to tell Oswald that he had prayed about the matter and felt led to give him a check for $20,000.00 with no strings attached. I'll never forget Oswald's amazement when I told him what Mr. Jaffray had said. It was a real lesson for the congregation and a better one for me."

It may have been coincidental that Jaffray's brother Robert was an outstanding missionary in China with the Christian and Missionary Alliance. Regardless of what prompted his interest Smith was sincerely grateful. Within a very short time the building was purchased and The Peoples Church and Oswald Smith had a permanent address.

The purchase of the church caused a stir in Toronto and the papers picked up the story. The three dailies were always fair in their treatment of articles about the work, or Smith in particular. The reporters were as professional as the editorial policy. If it was news, it was reported, honestly and objectively. If questions needed to be answered, they were asked. Because of Smith's orthodox approach, everything was out in the open. This included published audited financial statements at the end of each fiscal year in *The Peoples Magazine*.

No matter how much you disclose about your affairs it is never enough for some people. In this case it was Toronto's two "sensational" weekly tabloids which depended on the spectacular and sordid for their copy. For nine years Smith, The Peoples Church, and many of the visiting evangelists were fair game. The editors went about as far as they could go within the bounds of libel. Their readers were fed a constant stream of innuendos, particularly in the area of financial chicanery. As a result, their papers sold.

The "so-called" crusade against religion had two significant results. First, it caused people to think and talk about religion in general and The Peoples Church in particular. On more than one occasion, Smith had total strangers come into his office and congratulate him on what he was doing. They told him that they had lost all respect for the editorial standards of the publications. Some even went so far as to make a donation to the work as evidence of their good faith. Secondly, it resulted in Smith's most cherished motto, "No Attack . . . No Defense." Many outraged members of his congregation literally demanded that he answer the accusations, either from the pulpit or in civil court. He absolutely refused.

"I knew that it would be useless to take them to court. The editors were intelligent men and knew exactly how far they could go and still keep from being sued for slander. I'd just be playing into their hands if I took action — and I realized it. Besides, they were really doing me and the work a favor. The Peoples Church became known by a segment of the community who wouldn't even give it, or any church, a second look. It also gained sympathy because many people like to champion an underdog. Some eventually came to the services out of curiosity and I know that they could never say they hadn't heard the Gospel."

Smith's experience with Jaffray and his generosity was just one of the many examples of the type of people who were attracted to the work and made contributions of either a personal or financial nature. It would be impossible to list everyone who has made their presence felt down through the years. There are, however, six who deserve singular mention.

For nearly ten years, from 1943 to the early 50's, Smith had as his Associate Pastor Dr. P. W. Philpott who is best remembered as: the founder of The Philpott Tabernacle in Hamilton; builder and pastor of the new 4,000 seat Moody Church in Chicago and pastor of The Church of the Open Door in Los Angeles. Those years of working together with this man are among Smith's most cherished memories.

A. G. Malcolm was Vice-President of Gordon Mackay & Company Limited of Toronto and one of Smith's closest confidantes and loyal supporters. His association began with The Alliance Tabernacle and continued through to Bloor Street until his death.

Miss Alice Porter was Smith's Deaconess for 25 years. He relied on her efficient, prayerful support. Not being what you would term a "visiting" minister, Smith channeled many of the personal contacts through her. She was an outstanding woman and for years was an integral part of the work.

The most difficult thing to do, at this point is to pick out one person over another, because each one made their presence felt and contributed. Some, because of personal desire or circumstances, were more prominent and Smith needed these people. The real backbone of his work, however, were the behind-the-scenes faithful who prayed, gave and worked without recognition or praise.

Wilbert C. Willis was such a one, a tireless worker and friend who stood by Smith from The Alliance Tabernacle, through the work on Gerrard Street, and finally until his passing while a member at Bloor Street. "He was my right arm," is the way Smith describes Willis.

Music has always played a major role in Smith's ministry. Beginning with The Alliance Tabernacle one man has provided continuity in this area of the work. Practically every Sunday and weeknight service down through the years Donald Billings is at the grand piano. He is the perfect pianist because he uses his musical skills as an accompanist rather than as a featured artist. For nearly 30 years he has partnered Frank Trenchard who in the opinion of some is "the best organist in any evangelical church." The two musicians complement one another and work as a well-trained team. It is coincidental that Don Billings is also Smith's brother-in-law. "Family relationships do not enter into my reasons for attending Smith's church," he says. "I have a strong admiration for the man. We've been friends for years."

H. H. Phinnemore is a prime example of one of the countless faithful who have worked without public acclaim. He answered Smith's request for volunteers as ushers when the work was in Massey Hall. "He was the first man to respond so I made him my head usher," said Smith. "I've always stressed the importance of first impressions, especially with strangers. I feel that ushering can either make or break a congregation. Mr. Phinnemore is my idea of the perfect usher and all the years he was in charge, I never gave that area of the work a second thought. It was in good hands."

Phinnemore was also on the Board of Managers for a number of years until his retirement and elevation to the position of Honorary Board Member.

Because of its world-wide ministry, The Peoples Church has attracted the interest and support of numerous outside organizations and individuals. Jack McAlister and his World Literature Crusade have probably done as much, if not more, than anyone else to distribute Smith's books and enhance his reputation. By means of his radio broacasts McAlister has dispersed thousands of copies of Smith's works to every continent and practically every country. This international outreach has been possible because the books have been widely translated into many languages including: Arabic; Bengali; Chinese; Dutch; Finnish; French; German; Greek; Hindi; Japanese; Nepali; Swahili; Taiwanese; Vietnamese and numerous others.

In the early eighteenth century Charles Caleb Colton said, "Imitation is the sincerest form of flattery." This sage saying can be applied without question to The Peoples Church. Never before in Canadian religious history has a church and its techniques been imitated to such a degree. When Smith was at the zenith of his career whatever he attempted came under the close scrutiny of his contemporaries. Time after time, he would hear about various churches or evangelists attempting to duplicate his achievements. Sometimes they succeeded admirably, sometimes just moderately, and more often than not, they failed for some unexplained reason. This is not to say that everything Smith attempted turned out to be a resounding success. On the contrary, he had his fair share of disasters, as this book has pointed out. In three areas, however, he was unexcelled, and to this day no one has really reached his heights. He pioneered the Back Home Hour, popularized missionary conventions, and made faith promise offerings and evangelistic crusades common in Canada.

THE BACK HOME HOUR: this really became the first religious musical variety hour on Canadian radio. Sold on the idea that his congregation would respond to the best in music, he gave Eldon Lehman complete freedom to develop and produce an hour-long radio program. It was to be broadcast live from the main auditorium of the church, half an hour following the completion of the regular Sunday evening service.

"For six years we had what the manager of radio station CKNC called 'the finest variety hour on Canadian radio,'" recalled Lehman. "This was in direct competition with such popular programs as the Chase and Sanborn Hour with Charlie McCarthy. We didn't attempt to compete with these programs, rather we relied on our captive and built-in audience. Smith and I knew the audience we would be reaching on a Sunday so we made the most of the Christian listening habits of the day. Many wouldn't turn on their radios for anything but a religious program, so we decided to give them the best. This included the finest choir numbers, the best in orchestrations and whenever available, some of the outstanding Christian artists. The program always closed with Smith's fifteen-minute message.

"When we started, it was with the idea that the congregation would leave following the benediction and hurry home to tune in the program. This never happened, for they wanted to stay for the broadcast. We conducted a survey and found out that nearly 90 per cent of the congregation stayed; only those with small children left. Sometimes members of the choir and orchestra with families took turns taking the children home so at least one could take part in the broadcast. This presented real problems as the program caught on. Members of other churches rushed down to catch the broadcast and practically every Sunday evening literally hundreds were turned away. Smith was warned many times by the fire department that he was breaking the law by packing in so many people. They used to stand along the walls and sit in the aisles. It became so bad that he had to make an announcement over the radio during the Sunday broadcast of the regular service, for the people to stay away and listen on the radio. It was fantastic. They still came and the Fire Marshal threatened, but he never did anything about it.

"Smith never really knew what the program would be until it was presented. I suppose that his confidence in my ability was reflected in the success we enjoyed. Whatever it was, the response from the radio audience was remarkable. It was not uncommon for us to receive hundreds of letters every week. Many would be in the form of requests or testimonials of special blessings. The program was extremely popular with the infirm and shut-ins. It would be impossible to produce the same thing today. I've never really heard of anyone before or since coming close to duplicating The Back Home Hour."

Missionary Conventions: since foreign missions is Smith's greatest passion and interest, it is to be expected that the highlight of his church year was the Annual Missionary Convention.

"I've always stressed foreign missions at the expense of the home base," explained Smith. "While I never really pinpointed the variance in percentages a check of the disbursements of all the monies received by the church shows that down through the years, an average of 80 per cent or more was channeled into the missionary budget and 20 per cent or less for the home base or church expenses."

Smith's policy in the area of missionaries and societies is clear-cut and unmistakable. He formulated a set of conditions and has adhered to them down through the years. This has resulted in very little friction or misunderstanding.

The Peoples Church Missionary Policy

1) Each year a missionary convention is held at which time a faith promise offering is taken for the next twelve months. Only societies who have missionaries supported by the church are invited.
2) Speakers are invited upon the understanding that no direct or indirect solicitation of the congregation will be made.
3) Missionaries are accepted for support upon the under-

standing that they will make no appeal for their extra
needs.

4) Only missionaries of societies accredited by the Inter-
denominational Foreign Mission Association of North
America are supported.

5) The various societies are encouraged to assign missionaries
for support.

6) No attempt is made to administer the work on any of the
fields. All arrangements are made between the church and
society.

7) $1,200 is contributed annually to a married couple. No
provision is made for transportation, equipment or special
needs on the field.

8) Cooperation with the societies is centered around those
concentrating on reaching the two thousand unevangelized
tribes of the earth.

9) Physical needs are not emphasized with congregations.
All efforts are directed to appealing on a spiritual level.

10) Commitments to the missionaries, through the societies,
are limited to twelve months. These are renewed following each missionary convention provided that sufficient
funds have been promised.

11) Payments are continued for one year following the missionary's return home on furlough. If the missionary does
not return to the field following twelve months the responsibility ceases.

12) The Peoples Church supports only Canadian missionaries.
Allowances commence with the first quarter following
the missionary's departure and then follow on a regular
quarterly basis.

13) A significant portion of the total missionary offering is
channeled toward a program of foreign literature
disbursement.

14) It is a practice to work closely with the Faith-Missions or
societies because they do not major on institutional education or medical work.

15) Contributions are not made out of sympathy but, rather,
are based on field needs.

16) Home missions are recognized as important but are not
supported because The Peoples Church is geared to a program of foreign missions.

17) Natives are not supported because it is the opinion that
this is the responsibility of the host nation.

18) Missions or societies with low overhead are considered to
be of prime importance simply because a larger percent-
age of the missionary dollar reaches the field.

By maintaining this approach, Smith has personally raised approximately $14 million for foreign missions. This includes nearly $7 million in his own church and the balance in churches of all denominations in North America. It should be pointed out that the money Smith raises in other churches does not come under his control or influence. Each church or organization is responsible for the administration of its own program and Smith does not enter into the picture in any way. He is merely the expert, or figurehead, who is brought into the church because of his unique ability in the field of raising vast sums for missions.

Unlike some churches who concentrate on just a few missionaries and undertake their full support, Smith has always felt that The Peoples Church benefits greatly from a diverse budget. Since the missionary roster is enlarged, more fields are represented as well as missionary societies. This gives greater scope to the overall program, especially during the convention.

In a changing world the list of countries which even permit active missionary programs is never static. Open fields are closed, sometimes overnight. New areas of opportunity appear, as emerging nations with new identities and even names, recognize the value of missions both socially and economically.

During 1968, The Peoples Church contributed to the support of 326 missionaries who were registered with 35 faith mission boards and were serving on 21 major fields including: Arabia; British Guiana; Central America; Fiji Islands; India; Indonesia; Japan; Malaya; Mexico; Pakistan; Panama; Philippines; Singapore; South America; Taiwan; Thailand and the West Indies.

Some years the missionary roster has risen as high as 360 missionaries. The fluctuation was caused by economic or personnel demands. The overall program has also undergone changes in the last few years. This is necessary because it has to be contemporary and meet current conditions.

Being completely international in scope has meant that Smith has been able to keep his congregations enthused. He has symbolically brought the four corners of the globe onto the platform . . . many times in native costume.

The missionary societies responded to this approach because it is prestigious to be able to say that "we are a Peoples Church missionary." This identification assists with deputation work and the solicitating of additional support from unrelated congregations.

The responsibility of meeting financial commitments of well over $300,000.00 every year, has stimulated Smith to develop a technique of raising money and at the same time retain the respect of his congregations. This is not an easy undertaking. One has to tread lightly in this area because the risk of being branded a "money-grabbing "preacher is always present. His success reflects the close attention he has paid to this sensitive area of church work.

A typical missionary convention could be summed up in one word — "saturation." The convention usually ran for four weeks and five Sundays. There are meetings every week night and sometimes four on Sunday. They begin with the morning service followed by an afternoon, evening and closing service which runs from 9:00 to 10:00 p.m. The balconies and walls of the main auditorium are draped with banners carrying many of Smith's mottos which he sprinkles in most of his missionary sermons. He has always found that mottos repeated over and over again are an excellent means of educating a congregation. Some of his more popular ones are "The mission of the church is missions"; "The Gospel must first be published among all nations"; "You can't take it with you, but you can send it on ahead"; and probably his most famous, "Why should anyone hear the Gospel twice before everyone has heard it once?"

The missionaries and societies are invited to set up displays in the secondary auditorium. These exhibits become the focal point of interest between the services. It gives the missionaries and new candidates an opportunity to meet the people and it gives the people access to missionaries on a personal basis. Instead of just hearing the missionaries from the platform, the people are able to talk to them personally in an informal atmosphere. So that many will be encouraged to remain for the Sunday afternoon service and then the evening program, refreshments are served.

The dominant feature of the main auditorium was the large

169

thermometer which was well over fifteen feet high. The missionary goal was at the top and graduated figures ran down the thermometer to the base. As the totals were announced a wide red ribbon was run up.

While the speakers, mottos, exhibit room and thermometer caught the eye it was the missionary faith-promise offering which formed the fulcrum on which the whole program balanced.

Smith would work the congregation up gradually and bring it along until the final Sunday when everyone was at an elevated pitch of excitement. Each service usually featured three missionary or society speakers, musical groups or soloists, plus films or slides every week night. Smith chaired every meeting bringing the overall goal before the congregation and the specific needs of one field after another. This all contributed to the faith-promise offering which he popularized. No one has ever duplicated his achievements in this area.

"Offerings are a touchy area with most church congregations," points out Smith. "Practically every evangelical minister stresses tithing and the Christian's responsibility. I knew that if I were to raise the money necessary to carry out a missionary program, a new approach would be needed. That is when I hit upon the idea of faith-promises. I figured that most would respond to a promise that would be a private matter just between themselves and God. They would be asked to make it in complete dependency that God would undertake in this matter. This relieved them of the fear of having anyone embarrass them because of an unsatisfied promise. They'd never be asked for it! It has worked because there has never been a year that the total amount hasn't come in. In fact, we always seem to get more than was promised at the convention. This is probably due to people underestimating their potential at the time."

Special envelopes are made up and squares printed alongside monthly figures ranging from $2.00 to $100.00. There are blanks left at the top and bottom for less than $2.00 or more than $100.00. Everyone in the congregation is encouraged to take an envelope regardless of whether they have filled in one or not. This results in as many as three or four extra envelopes coming in from the same person or family.

As the envelopes are collected they are brought to the front of the auditorium where volunteers, sitting at small tables, extend the monthly figures into yearly totals and hand the envelopes to Smith. During the handing out and processing of the envelopes Smith paces back and forth, impatiently waiting to begin, what for him, is the most exciting phase of his ministry.

As the envelopes are completed he calls out the totals, never mentioning the name, just the totals. He builds suspense by removing what he calls "dessert" from the pile of envelopes. He considers anything over $600.00 a year dessert and holds back on these until the lower amounts have been called out. This is a good psychological move as it holds the interest. He also keeps the spirit of the service high with his jocular mood. As the dessert is called out the congregation responds with loud "Amens" or "Praise God." Congregational singing and special musical numbers back up the program. Sometimes Smith will have the people stand and sing "Bringing In Chinese" or "Bringing Hindus In" to the tune of "Bringing in the Sheaves."

Once all the envelope totals are called out and the grand total ready the people are asked to stand. It is an exciting moment as Smith announces the figure and the thermometer is run up. It is not uncommon for the congregation to break into applause before singing the Doxology. At the final service, when the grand total is announced, the entire congregation joins with the choir and orchestra to sing the Hallelujah Chorus as the ribbon is run up and the thermometer broken, indicating that another goal has been exceeded.

Conventions such as the one described above are not peculiar to The Peoples Church. While Smith will readily admit that it is in his own church where he has had his greatest triumphs, he has been eminently successful elsewhere.

One church which invited him back five times after the initial conference was the Park Street Church in Boston, Massachusetts, where Dr. Harold J. Ockenga was the minister.

"Park Street owes a debt to Oswald J. Smith and I am

happy to acknowledge that debt," wrote Dr. Ockenga. "At my suggestion he was first invited in 1938 to hold a Victory Life Campaign. During his visit we talked over the possibility of holding a missionary conference, something never before attempted in the church's 135-year history. I decided that we should have one and booked him for the Spring of 1940. He conducted the conference in the same manner as he does in his own church and the results were outstanding. The total raised by the faith-promise offering was $21,339.00. This was in sharp contrast to the previous year's missionary giving of just $9,043.00.

"Dr. Smith was invited to return for the next five conferences, and the amounts increased to: $32,703 in 1941; $33,387 in 1942; $47,753 in 1943; $52,988 in 1944 and $57,771 in 1945. This came to a total of $235,941 under his leadership.

"The Park Street Church now has an annual missionary budget of well over $300,000. We are grateful to Dr. Smith for giving this church the vision of missions and showing us how to heed God's great commission."

EVANGELISTIC CRUSADES: "I wouldn't like to be placed in the position of singling out one preacher or crusade over the other. Each man had something that sets him apart," said Smith. "Jackie Burris, for example, had a superior gift for putting on his own campaigns. He never relied on the cooperation of a number of churches. He just went to a city where he thought God would use him and began his crusade. He rented the auditoriums, bought space in the papers and time on radio for advertising. He invited any minister in the area who might like to cooperate but that's as far as it went. He controlled everything. He didn't hold campaigns for others, he held them for himself. In the case of his memorable campaign in The Peoples Church, which culminated in two mass Sunday evening services in Maple Leaf Gardens, he worked closely with me. Those two services drew over 11,000 people and were the greatest religious meetings ever held in Maple Leaf Gardens up to that time. Because of our missionary program Burris caught the vision and went on a tour to a number of foreign fields. He was a great evangelist.

"Another noted evangelist who came to The Peoples Church was Henry Grube of Mobile, Alabama. Grube has returned more times to the pulpit of the church than any other person. I think the figure now stands at just over 25 separate appearances. He is a great preacher and Bible teacher. I would often turn the pulpit over to him for weeks at a time while I was away on some missionary or evangelistic trip.

"I consider myself fortunate to have been exposed to some of the greatest pulpiteers of the twentieth century. A number of names come to mind, but only two stand out above all others . . . Paul Rader and Dr. William Hogg. Both men were remarkable and I've never seen congregations moved to such an extent before or since, with the possible exception of Billy Graham whom I rate as the best of them all. In the field of evangelism there is only one man who really stands out among the greats. He is Gypsy Smith. This man had crowd appeal. What he might have lacked in formal education he more than made up for it in sheer personal magnetism. Anyone who recalls the campaigns he held in The Peoples Church and in Massey Hall will, I am sure, agree with me."

One such a person was William Douglas who was only ten years old when Gypsy Smith held his campaign.

"I remember it well," recalled Douglas. "I was in the junior choir at the time which was led by Jess Pike. We had been practicing for weeks and were excited at the thought of being on the platform of Massey Hall. We were to sing with the church choir and orchestra under the direction of Eldon Lehman who was fascinating to watch in action.

"We were part of the service for four consecutive Sunday nights in Massey Hall and for a kid of ten, it was quite a thrill. The auditorium was packed with many people standing for every service. There were over 300 children and adults in the mass choir plus the orchestra. I remember watching Dr. Smith as he conducted the service and wondered how he ever remembered what to do or say. To a child, he was an impressive, remotely distant person who was always preoccupied about something. There was never any doubt about the fact that it was his service and he was in complete charge.

"Gypsy Smith was an old man of 80 at that time, but he

had a remarkable vitality. He would prance back and forth holding his Bible in one hand and grinning from ear to ear under a bushy moustache. When it came time to give the invitation he was all business. During his sermons he would tell stories of his life in the Gypsy caravans in England and look around at us kids on the platform with a twinkle in his eye. 'Better watch out,' he'd grin. 'Gypsies have been known to steal little children.' We all liked him and for children were attentive. Perhaps we sat still because our parents were out in the audience and warned us well not to fidget, at least mine did.

"I never knew until years later that I had been part of one of the greatest campaigns in the history of The Peoples Church or Massey Hall, for that matter. I understand from a story published in *The Peoples Magazine* that a total of 921 decisions were registered, including 440 young people, 431 adults, and 50 children. For me it was a unique experience and I've never been a part of anything since which has left such an impression."

The success of the Gypsy Smith Campaign was the result of long hours and hard work by many people. For this undertaking there were 225 active participants excluding those in the musical program. In addition, a full scale promotion was conducted. Smith announced the crusade and stimulated interest and enthusiasm as only he could do. Space was purchased in the papers and on radio so that by the time the meetings began everyone (those connected with an evangelical church at least) knew what was happening. So that other churches would cooperate by acknowledging the meetings Smith invited as many ministers as possible to sit on the platform and speak before the main messages.

Not every campaign was conducted on such an extensive scale. All, however, received the full benefit of Smith's promotional skills. If he had not been sold on mass meetings as a means of reaching the lost with the Gospel they would have failed. As it was, the people came, night after night, week after week, for a continual diet of one campaign after the other.

So successful was Smith at drawing crowds that he had

to cease all newspaper advertising for a seven year period. The Fire Marshal issued constant warnings about the overcrowded conditions of the main auditorium. In an effort to cooperate Smith limited his promotions to his congregation only. It didn't make much difference, because the church was continually packed with many standing along the walls. It was a common occurrence for the doors to be closed before the meetings started and many turned away.

It is an accepted fact that those days have passed. Television, travel and affluence have relegated such times to antiquity. While they lasted, souls were saved and a vacuum was filled in many lives. For a large segment of the community the church and its changing program was all they had to look forward to in the otherwise dull and monotonous existence of the depression years.

Chapter 15

Years from now, when Oswald J. Smith has passed from the scene, his memory will still live on. His place in religious history will not have been earned especially, by his accomplishments as a minister, evangelist, missionary leader or author, but rather as a hymnist.

Of the more than twelve hundred hymns and poems he has written over the years, several stand as having gained a niche in the list of twentieth century greats.

In 1934 he composed "The Glory of His Presence." Recalling the circumstances which surrounded the writing of the poem he said, "It came to me in the middle of the night and was written as an expression of a deeply moving experience. It highlights failure, disappointment and restoration. When B. D. Ackley wrote the music and I first heard it sung I knew that God had given me the words to what I was sure would become a well-known hymn."

The Glory of His Presence

I have walked alone with Jesus
    In a fellowship divine;
Never more can earth allure me,
    I am His and He is mine.

Chorus
I have seen Him, I have known Him,
    For He deigns to walk with me;
And the glory of His presence will be mine eternally.
    O the glory of His presence, O the beauty of His face;
I am His and His forever, He has won me by His grace.

The 1930's were Smith's most productive years, as far as his best known hymns are concerned. It was during that decade that four of his finest songs were written.

In 1934 Smith's youngest sister, Ruth, and her husband, Reverend Clifford Bicker, were preparing to leave Peru to return home on their first furlough from the mission field. Just before their boat was to sail Clifford was instantly killed in an automobile accident.

As Ruth stepped off the train in Toronto with her two small children, Smith was overcome by the tragedy. In an effort to offer some comfort to his sister he dedicated his newest hymn, "God Understands."

GOD UNDERSTANDS

God understands your sorrow,
    He sees the falling tear,
And whispers, "I am with thee,"
    Then falter not, nor fear.
Chorus
He understands your longing,
    Your deepest grief He shares;
Then let Him bear your burden,
    He understands, and cares.

"The Song of the Soul Set Free" is Smith's greatest choir number. None other lends itself so well to full orchestration. On many occasions it has been sung by the mass choirs of the Billy Graham Crusades and was a featured number of the R.C.A. Victor album recorded at Graham's Sydney, Australia, Crusade. George Beverly Shea took the solo part accompanied by the choir under the leadership of Cliff Barrows.

"When A. H. Ackley sent me the original manuscript, his music sang itself into my heart," recalls Smith. "Before too long I had the first verse, then the chorus and the balance of the hymn. It really wrote itself once I had decided upon the theme which was to exalt the Lord Jesus Christ every way possible."

THE SONG OF THE SOUL SET FREE

Fairest of ten thousand, is Jesus Christ my Saviour,
    The Lily of the Valley, the Bright and Morning Star,
He is all my glory and in this heart of mine,
    Forevermore I'm singing a song of love divine.

Chorus
'Tis the song of the soul set free,
    And its melody is ringing;
'Tis the song of the soul set free,
    Joy and peace to me it's bringing,
'Tis the song of the soul set free,
    And my heart is ever singing
Hallelujah! Hallelujah!
    The song of the soul set free!

"During May of 1939 I was staying at the Headquarters of The China Inland Mission in Philadelphia and took the opportunity to visit my friend and musical colleague, B. D. Ackley. We were chatting by his piano when Homer Rodeheaver came in and said, 'I want a hymn depicting the change that took place in the lives of men when Jesus came.' Rodeheaver went on at great length describing what he had in mind, then left.

"The following day I wrote the words to 'Then Jesus Came' and gave it to Rodeheaver who composed the beautiful music. The rest is history. This has, in my estimation, become the best known of all my hymns. Perhaps the fact that George Beverly Shea recorded it as a solo for one of his R.C.A. Victor albums has helped. It was really well established before he became so prominent. In any case, I'm grateful that it is being used so widely and that God has blessed it so richly. I know of many ministers who use it as an invitation hymn. I could not ask for anything more."

THEN JESUS CAME
One sat alone beside the highway begging,
    His eyes were blind, the light he could not see;
He clutched his rags and shivered in the shadows,
    Then Jesus came and bade his darkness flee.

Chorus
When Jesus comes the tempter's power is broken;
    When Jesus comes the tears are wiped away.
He takes the gloom and fills the life with glory,
    For all is changed when Jesus comes to stay.

Since Smith is an individualist and not particularly identified with one denomination or position, he is sometimes challenged on his stand. There has never been any equivocation as to his Biblical position. Aligning himself solidly behind the Evangelical viewpoint, he firmly accepts the Bible as the inspired Word of God and its contents literally, except when the Bible clearly indicates that the passage is parabolic or allegoric. He is in complete opposition to the thinking that the Bible only contains the Word of God and that many of its stories are just fables with strong moral or spiritual truths. For him, Jonah and the big fish, Daniel in the lion's den, Moses and the Red Sea, the feeding of the five thousand, and the turning of water into wine are just as real as the Virgin Birth, the crucifixion, or the Lord's bodily resurrection. Smith firmly believes that Christ ascended into Heaven on a cloud only to return some day in the same way. These are firmly implanted in his mind and for sixty years he has never wavered from such fixed positions.

"Many times, when I'm away from home I'm asked to state my stand on prophecy," says Smith. "I've always been a pre-millennialist and make no apologies for it. I could never, in the light of Biblical evidence, accept either the post-millennialist or a-millennialist theories.

"For a Bible, I use a Scofield Reference and rely on the many other fine translations for additional background and inspiration. My son Paul, prefers the Thompson Chain Reference Bible and we kid each other about it much to the amusement of the congregation. It is just a matter of preference, but I've found it best to choose one and stick with it."

Definite as Smith's views are on prophecy and the Bible, so is his approach to personal finances.

"In all modesty, I could have been comfortably situated by now if I had treated finances in the same manner as many do," stated Smith. "For years all I've ever accepted in the way of a salary from The Peoples Church was a flat $5,000.00. This was in the face of the Board of Managers' insistence that I accept more in view of my responsibilities as minister. They felt that a church with a missionary budget of well over $300 thousand, plus an ambitious church program, should pay its minister more than one percent of the gross income.

"While I've always enjoyed comfortable surroundings, I've

never wasted money. I've always felt that the Lord's work came first. I would never have felt right about appealing for large missionary offerings if I took a large salary for myself. It has always been easier to stand before a congregation and ask them to give sacrificially when I wasn't taking anything more than my basic needs required.

"As far as my books are concerned I've never personally gained from either the writing or sale of them. I made an arrangement with my publisher, Marshall, Morgan and Scott, to waive all royalties on my books if they would pro rate the money into the production costs. This permitted them to keep the cost and sale price down so that they were in the reach of everyone. The church has benefited from the arrangement and this is what I wanted. When you consider that I've written 35 books which have had a combined circulation of over 3 million copies in 70 languages, you can appreciate that even at a modest royalty I'd have enjoyed a sizable return even on the English editions."

Once World War Two was over and the country had returned to some form of normalcy, Smith was on the move again. Taking up where he left off in 1939 before international travel was restricted, he embarked upon a heavy schedule of world tours.

His most extensive pre-war trip was in 1938 during which he visited Hawaii, Samoa, Fiji, Australia, the Solomon Islands and New Zealand. His first-hand reports and colorful pictures of that romantic part of the globe stimulated a wave of interest in missions never before experienced in The Peoples Church. Besides the encouragement he brought to missionaries as he visited them on the field, he was instrumental in revitalizing evangelism particularly in Australia.

Alex Gilchrist of Sydney, Australia, remembered Smith's 1938 crusade in his city. "It was my father-in-law, 'Cairo' Bradley, and Canon R. B. S. Hammond, who were instrumental in inviting Dr. Smith to hold a series of crusades in Australia.

"The services were held in the major cities of the country and the crowds were beyond expectation. Dr. Smith introduced several new approaches to evangelizing. The most effective and best remembered was his technique of having trained counselors and a practical method of dealing with those who responded to the invitation. He is also responsible for giving to many of the Australian churches a vision for missions. Many who responded to his call to the foreign field are presently active in missions today. Dr. Smith placed the need of New Guinea and Papua before the crusade audiences. When I visited those fields recently, I met some of the men and women who responded and became full-time missionaries to those needy people."

In a life of highlights it is difficult to isolate one over another but on June 14, 1936, Smith experienced the greatest thrill of his ministry up to that time.

"One of my Christian heros was Charles Haddon Spurgeon. I have read practically all of his major writings and he has been a source of great inspiration to me down through the years. It's impossible to express my feelings at being invited to preach from his pulpit in the world-famous Spurgeon's Tabernacle in London, England, for a few Sundays beginning in June of 1936."

All in all, Smith has made 19 world tours and visited 72 countries on 6 continents. Each one of his trips stand out because of where he visited, who he saw, or the sermons he preached. Two, however, are worthy of special note and are probably his most memorable.

In 1955, along with his wife, he toured South Africa and held services in most of the major cities plus many out-of-the-way mission stations. His itinerary covered: Senegal; Liberia; the Gold Coast; Congo; Anglo-Egyptian Sudan; Egypt; Southern Rhodesia and South Africa.

The Dutch Reformed Church of South Africa, in particular, is not noted for its wide-open approach to evangelism. It is a staid, respectable, state church which preaches the Gospel with as little fan fare as possible. Smith's brand of soul-saving stirred up the people. The results, which are still being talked about by those who attended the meetings, were completely foreign to anything they had experienced up to that time.

Smith also infused new life into their sagging missionary program. One report from a reliable source in South Africa revealed that the overall missionary giving of the Dutch Reformed Church had risen by thousands of pounds annually since Smith's visit.

The most remarkable tour of all and the highlight of Smith's oversea's crusades took place in 1957 when he and his wife traveled to South America. Mrs. E. Spitzer, a South American missionary, personally organized eight city-wide campaigns in most of the capital cities of: Brazil, Argentina, Uruguay, Chile, Peru, Ecuador, Colombia and Panama. For the first time in history all the Protestant churches united together in a common bond and completely cooperated in supporting the crusades.

The original crowd estimates were modest because the meetings were in predominantly Roman Catholic countries, but on one occasion they exceeded 25,000. According to the police of Buenos Aires, Argentina, more than 5,000 were turned away from one of the meetings in that city. Following the crusades the organizers reported that just over 4,500 first-time decisions for salvation were registered.

Smith has no set formula for instant success. Many times, from the pulpit, he has expressed amazement at what God has permitted him to do. He openly realizes his limitations and candidly admits that if it had been left up to him he probably would have ended his days as a run-of-the-mill preacher in some small charge.

"It's not false modesty," he points out, "just a simple statement of fact. If I hadn't kept close to God all these years I'm sure I'd never have amounted to anything."

This closeness to God took the form of what Smith calls his "Morning Watch." Every morning he spends at least an hour, sometimes more, alone in his study with his thoughts and God. The first half hour is spent reading the Bible and meditating. The balance is spent in prayer. It is not the usual quiet prayer that one associates with early morning. Rather, it's a conversational prayer. He talks to God out loud as if he were talking to someone in the study with him. Since he considers God to be an integral part of his life this approach is not unexpected. In addition to praying out loud he walks back and forth. This he feels, keeps him active and his mind alert.

"For over fifty years I've never missed a 'Morning Watch,' states Smith. "The only time I've broken the pattern is when I've been sick in bed and could not raise my head. When those days were upon me I prayed flat on my back. This is a part of my life and something that is as important to me as sleeping and eating.

"I state without reservation, that it has been the 'Morning Watch,' more than any other single thing, that has contributed to any success God has permitted me to achieve."

The walls of Smith's office and study are dotted with pictures and honors bestowed on him over a long and illustrious career. While he has never been granted an earned degree, he has been the recipient of a number of honorary degrees, none of which were ever solicited:

1936   Doctor of Divinity — Asbury Seminary

1939   Life Member of the Royal Geographical Society of London

1940   Doctor of Literature — Bob Jones University

1940   Member of the Eugene Field Society (National Association of Authors and Journalists)

1946   Doctor of Laws — Houghton College

1952   Member of the Royal Society of Literature of the United Kingdom

1953   Member of the American Society of Composers and Authors

Not all of Smith's waking hours are devoted to church and religion. In the "golden age of radio" his favorite program was "Amos and Andy." With the coming of television, he never misses "Death Valley Days" unless it is absolutely unavoidable. He has been known to refuse telephone calls when these programs were on, something he never does under normal circumstances. His early years in the Canadian west probably account for his interest in one of television's finest western shows.

Ever since he was a child he has always had an interest in birds and animals. For a number of years the sunroom in his home was turned into a giant aviary which was filled with a wide selection of parakeets and African finches.

For most people, travel such as the kind Smith has undertaken is completely out of the question. Realizing that he was fortunate to see many exotic places he took up photography and became quite proficient. He has an excellent collection of 35 millimeter slides and 16 millimeter colored film. Both are used to great advantage especially with congregations during missionary conventions. Many agree that he has one of the finest collections of missionary films and slides in existence. There may be more in-depth collections on one particular area, but it is doubtful if there are many more extensive.

The problem of succession always faces someone who founds a business or some form of public organization. Smith's situation was no different. His personal dream was to have one of his sons follow in his footsteps. The question was solved by his eldest son, Glen, in no uncertain terms.

Paul remembers the occasion clearly. "One evening while Glen and I were lying on our beds talking about nothing in particular he turned over and looked me straight in the eye. 'You know, Paul,' he said, 'Dad expects one of us to be a minister.'

"I had no idea what he was leading up to so all I could say was, yes I know. Without any preamble or explanation he stated in his matter-of-fact way, 'Well, you know, I'm not cut out for it at all.' That was all there was to it. He flopped over on his back and picked up the conversation where he had left off. By virtue of the process of elimination I was chosen to become the second generation in the pulpit." Glen chose medicine as a career and is now one of Vancouver, British Columbia's leading gynecologists.

On January 1, 1959, Smith resigned as minister of The Peoples Church in favor of his son Paul who had already earned a reputation as one of Canada's leading new clerics and evangelists.

"I fought the pulpit of The Peoples Church for years," said Paul. "I wanted no part of it because I seriously doubted that anyone else could ever fill his shoes. I've tried to steer my own course and I can honestly say that Father has been a tremendous help. His comments are always positive and enthusiastic and have given me the lift I needed many times when things were rough."

Smith, as only a proud father would, rates his son highly. "Paul is a great Bible teacher and I always knew that he would leave his mark in the field of evangelism. He knows how to relate current events and how to present them in the light of Biblical revelation. This is something I've never been able to do with much success. He reaches the young people and they seem to respond. All you have to do is look over the congregation when he is preaching to see the number of young people he attracts. This is good because we are living in a young environment. I'm from another age."

Instead of retiring to his birds and photography, Smith embarked upon yet another career. He was designated Minister of Missions of The Peoples Church and President of The Peoples Missionary Society. This new-found freedom from administrative responsibilities allowed him to pursue his missionary and evangelistic ministry with greater intensity than ever before. At an age when most men are content to sit back in the reflected glory of bygone days, Smith is constantly amazing men of half his years with his vitality and enthusiasm. As he nears his eightieth birthday, his preaching has never been more fervent. Those who have sat under his ministry down through the years are firmly convinced that his messages are improving with age.

On January 2, 1959, he preached sermon number 9,601 in the pulpit of The Peoples Church. By January 1, 1969, the total had risen to 11,442 as he preached on "God's Three Men" in Fresno, California.

His calendar is solidly booked as far ahead as eighteen months. He has missionary conferences and evangelistic crusades scheduled throughout North America and as far away as Mexico and Denmark. If he accepted all the invitations extended to him, he would be on the go fifty-two weeks a year.

The only concession to advancing years is his close attention to his physical and emotional health. Whenever he travels, it is usually in the company of his wife. He paces himself carefully, reserving all his surplus energy for the pulpit. His days are usually left free and he keeps his social engagements down to a minimum, preferring to spend his free hours in rest and preparation. By maintaining a rigid schedule of rest and a balanced diet, he enjoys remarkable health . . . especially for a person who was never expected to reach maturity!

In addition to his speaking engagements he edits *The Peoples Magazine* four times a year and administers the world-wide literature program of the church. Sometimes, when the minister, Paul Smith, is away he assists with the preaching or conducts the meetings.

No one has ever accused Smith of being two people. He is always the same on the platform or off. His intense concentration, which he directs to one thing, the work of the Lord and missions in particular, excludes everything else. He has, because of this dedication, accomplished more than many who divide their attention between the church, the Lord, and their family.

Those who know him personally defend any implication that he is without humor or personal feeling.

"My father," says his daughter, Hope, "is kind, sympathetic, humorous, generous and extremely affectionate.

"I remember an excellent example of when his preoccupation resulted in an extremely funny situation.

"It was after the benediction and Father had come off the platform. He saw me and shook hands warmly. I could hardly believe my ears when he asked me if I had enjoyed the service and hoped that I would come back again. He was so wrapped up in his own thoughts that he didn't even realize that I was his sixteen-year-old daughter."

His wife sees him through different eyes. "Oswald has always been very affectionate and generous. He has trusted me to carry out the responsibilities of the home. He may look severe, but it's only on the surface."

Smith reciprocates his wife's love and esteem. "If any sacrifices were made it was by my wife. She was the one who stayed at home and raised the children while I was on the move around the world. They, along with me, owe her a debt

186

which can never be repaid this side of Heaven. I could never have accomplished anything if I had not had her love and loyalty. She has been the perfect wife."

It has been said that "a man's butler knows the master best." Smith never had a butler, but he did have a close friend and confidante right in his home for many years. Before she passed on, Chrissie French was once asked what he was really like. "That man," she replied, "is more humble than the men who pick up our garbage." This is probably the finest tribute of them all . . . especially from one who was not given to superlatives.

One of Canada's most outspoken and controversial radio commentators is Gordon Sinclair of radio station CFRB, Toronto. He has long been an opponent of organized religion and has, on many occasions, lashed out at what he considers to be phonies and charlatans in the church today. He is, however, recognized as a fair person who responds to honesty and sincerity.

Besides his news and show business programs he has a featurette every day which highlights interesting subjects or personalities. One of his programs featured Smith and his ministry in the city of Toronto. It was a sympathetic piece and in closing Sinclair said, "While I don't agree with, nor can I accept, his brand of religion, I nevertheless respect him as an honest Christian gentleman."

Eldon B. Lehman, who worked with Smith during his crowning years, looks back on those days and his association as the greatest of his life.

"It is only natural," he says, "for Christian people to assess the accomplishments of outstanding ministers and evangelists in the light of such men as Moody, Torrey, Alexander, Billy Sunday, Paul Rader or Billy Graham. When they achieve some degree of prominence in comparison with the accomplishments of these men, they are branded as 'great.'

"I for one, who knew him so well, perhaps better than anyone else in those days, class Dr. Smith without reservation as one of the 'greats.'

"My greatest and lasting thrill was experienced Sunday after Sunday as I stood on the platform of The Peoples Church and watched God work through this man. We had tremendous times of great blessing. I am convinced that it was not necessary, in those days, to import evangelists or preachers to accomplish the same results. Oswald J. Smith was more than an equal to any of them. They were good and brought something to the congregation, but Smith was more than their match."

Just as the days of continuous evangelistic crusades were drawing to a close, so was the effective life of The Peoples Church at 100 Bloor Street East. Toronto was changing and moving out into the suburbs. With a population of close to 2 million in a large sprawling metropolis the trend was to a home church atmosphere. The downtown churches were quickly dying off and with one or two exceptions all the successful churches were moving away from the heart of the city along with their people.

Realizing that the time had come for a complete change in format and appearance, the new minister, Paul Smith, engineered and administered the sale of the church and the building of a new one in Willowdale, a northern suburb of the city.

On June 5, 1961, the old church was sold for $650,000. The new church was built and opened on October 28, 1962, completely debt-free. It has one of the finest auditoriums and physical plants in Ontario, if not the Dominion. Since that time the congregation has given almost half a million dollars for the construction of additional educational facilities. The Sunday congregation averages well over 2,000 for every service and the Sunday school has an average enrollment of over 1,500. A new elevation with seating for approximately another 200 was dedicated on Easter Sunday April 6, 1969.

In August of 1968 Smith left for a month-long series of evangelistic meetings in Australia and when he returned it was to the biggest surprise of his life.

"I wanted to recognize Father's sixtieth anniversary in the ministry in some unique way," said Paul. "For the church's 1967 'Centennial' project we commissioned Donald Inman, one of Canada's leading artists and designers, to construct a large wooden mural. It highlighted Father's career and is dominated by a three-times-bigger-than-life hand-carved profile of father in bas-relief. It now hangs in the foyer of the new Christian Education Wing which bears his name.

"The writing of his biography was also completely unexpected and something he had never really thought about. I had been considering it for some time because I didn't want it to be left until he was gone and unable to bask in some of the honor and esteem that was rightfully his.

"I knew that the one person who could really top his whole ministry off was Billy Graham, so I wrote him and asked if he could spare one night, any night of the year for a special service honoring Father. He immediately replied and suggested Tuesday evening, September 17th. He would be in Detroit that afternoon and said he would be delighted to fly into Toronto for four hours. That's all I needed and the greatest service in the history of the church was scheduled."

Smith was honestly embarrassed by the attention, but at the same time quietly pleased. "I was, of course, delighted that the church would dedicate the new 'Centennial' wing in my honor and have Don Inman design a plaque. The biography was completely unexpected and a wonderful thing to happen while I'm still alive to appreciate it. I never really thought about Billy Graham coming. It was the furthest thing from my mind.

"I remember the first time I ever had anything to do with Billy," said Smith. "It was shortly after the war in 1946 or '47. Charles B. Templeton was the minister of the Avenue Road Church at the time. He called me one day to see if I had an opening for a young North Carolina preacher who he thought might have promise. I checked my calendar and told him that everything was filled up with the exception of the young peoples meeting. Templeton thought it would be better than nothing so accepted the booking on behalf of his friend. I was curious to hear this man and see if Templeton was accurate in his evaluation, so I sat in on the meeting. There were about 40 or 50 present.

"Frankly I wasn't impressed. He didn't stand out particularly and I wasn't prompted to invite him back. Now look

Typical Sunday evening service at The Peoples Church

The new Peoples Church, Sheppard Ave., Toronto

at him. He is the greatest evangelist the world has ever known.

"When I returned from Australia and was told that Billy was coming, especially for me, it was the biggest thrill of my life."

Tuesday, September 17th, was a hot, humid day. The service had been publicized in the newspapers and in the church. Since Graham was bound by a tight schedule the service was scheduled for 7:00 o'clock. By three-thirty in the afternoon the lines began forming under a blazing sun. By the time the doors were opened the crowds had exceeded the total capacity of the main auditorium. A closed circuit television system was installed in the secondary auditoriums and these were also quickly filled. A conservative estimate by *The Telegram* placed the crowd at between 4,000 and 4,500.

Allen Spraggett, at that time Religion Editor of *The Toronto Daily Star* reported. "His (Graham's) VIP status was demonstrated during his visit to Toronto. He was met at the plane by an official of the airline and an RCMP officer and hustled through customs without the usual red tape.

"Introducing him at the service in The Peoples Church which was jammed by 4,000 in every nook and cranny, Dr. Oswald J. Smith called Billy Graham, 'One of the eight or ten best known people in the world,' and allowed that he considered his visit 'the greatest honor that has ever been bestowed on me or The Peoples Church.'"

As the platform party, led by Paul Smith, entered the auditorium, the congregation rose to their feet and gave Graham and Smith a standing ovation.

Following a medley of Smith's best known hymns by a 200 voice mass choir, Graham rose to speak.

"I have come to Toronto," he said, "for the express purpose of paying tribute to Dr. Oswald J. Smith, the founder of The Peoples Church."

He listed ten reasons why he thought Dr. Smith's ministry had been so successful during the past sixty years:

"1) He had an experience with Christ and he never got over it. He was soundly converted at the age of sixteen and is still talking about it.

2) He developed a love for the Word of God. He loves the Bible. He believes the Bible, and has never doubted its contents.

3) He maintained a discipline in his life. To write so many books, so many poems and preach so many sermons requires a disciplined mind. He also disciplines himself physically which accounts for his remarkable health.

4) He has always remained young. He has young people listening to him.

5) His home life backs up his public ministry. I don't think I've ever witnessed a greater father-son combination in the ministry.

6) He has a passion for souls. The characteristics of his ministry are a compassion and love for souls, a broken heart and complete dependence upon God.

7) He never got side-tracked. He just keeps right on with the Gospel and God has honored him with a long life and thousands of converts.

8) He has a social conscience because he believes that man must be changed if society is to be changed.

9) His missionary vision is contagious. He has repeated over and over again, 'the supreme task of the church is the evangelization of the world.' He believes in putting missions first and it has paid off.

10) He has maintained a love for God's people. He never got into mud-slinging contests. He might have disagreed with somebody but he did it in love. I have seen so many splits and divisions that I determined by God's grace that I was just going to keep on with the Gospel and love all the Lord's people, let the chips fall where they may. That is the way Oswald J. Smith has set the example and set the pace."

This then is the man who, if he had been made for defeat, would have quit years ago.